PURSUING PURPOSE

A Neuropsychological Approach to Maximize Life and Enjoy the Process

Nate Shanok, PhD

Praise for *Pursuing Purpose*

"The reader feels as though they are having a discussion with a trusted clinician who makes appropriate and helpful recommendations for discovering meaning and purpose. Even when discussing complicated subjects related to brain functioning or specific research studies, it is told in a way that is digestible to readers who do not have advanced degrees in neuropsychology." **—Viktor Frankl Institute of Logotherapy**

"A highly thorough and helpful approach."
—Alex Korb, Bestselling Author of The Upward Spiral

"It is absolutely worth it! *Pursuing Purpose* by Nate Shanok is a truly insightful read for those looking to get the most out of their lives. The book merges neuroscience, psychology, and practical advice to help readers understand their own potential and take action to achieve their desired life goals." **—Dr. Sukanlaya Sawang, Editor of Behavioral Sciences**

"Victor Frankl's ideas about people's search for purpose and meaning in life has been the bulwark for humanistic theory and psychotherapy. Rarely has it been examined from a neuropsychological perspective. This is what Nate Shanok has done in his highly accessible book, *Pursuing Purpose: A Neuropsychological Approach to Maximize Life and Enjoy the Process*. Dr. Shanok takes the reader on a personal journey of discovering purpose and its role in psychological wellbeing. Shanok combines descriptions of his own quest for purpose and those of others with rigorous scientific evaluations of the importance of purpose and meaning in psychological adjustment. The novel contribution of this book is the successful integration of humanistic theory and therapy influenced by Frankl's revolutionary ideas with solid empirical evidence, much of it neuropsychological. *Pursuing Purpose* will be of interest to anyone who has thought about the meaning of life (and whom of us hasn't) but who wants the answers to this existential question to be based on solid science."
—Dr. David Bjorklund, Author of Origins of the Social Mind: Evolutionary Psychology and Child Development

Pursuing Purpose

Nate Shanok, PhD, is the director of the Delray Center for Brain Science in Delray Beach, Florida. He specializes in the treatment of depression, anxiety, obsessive compulsive disorder, and existential crisis. He is also a professor in the Behavioral Sciences Department at Florida Atlantic University.

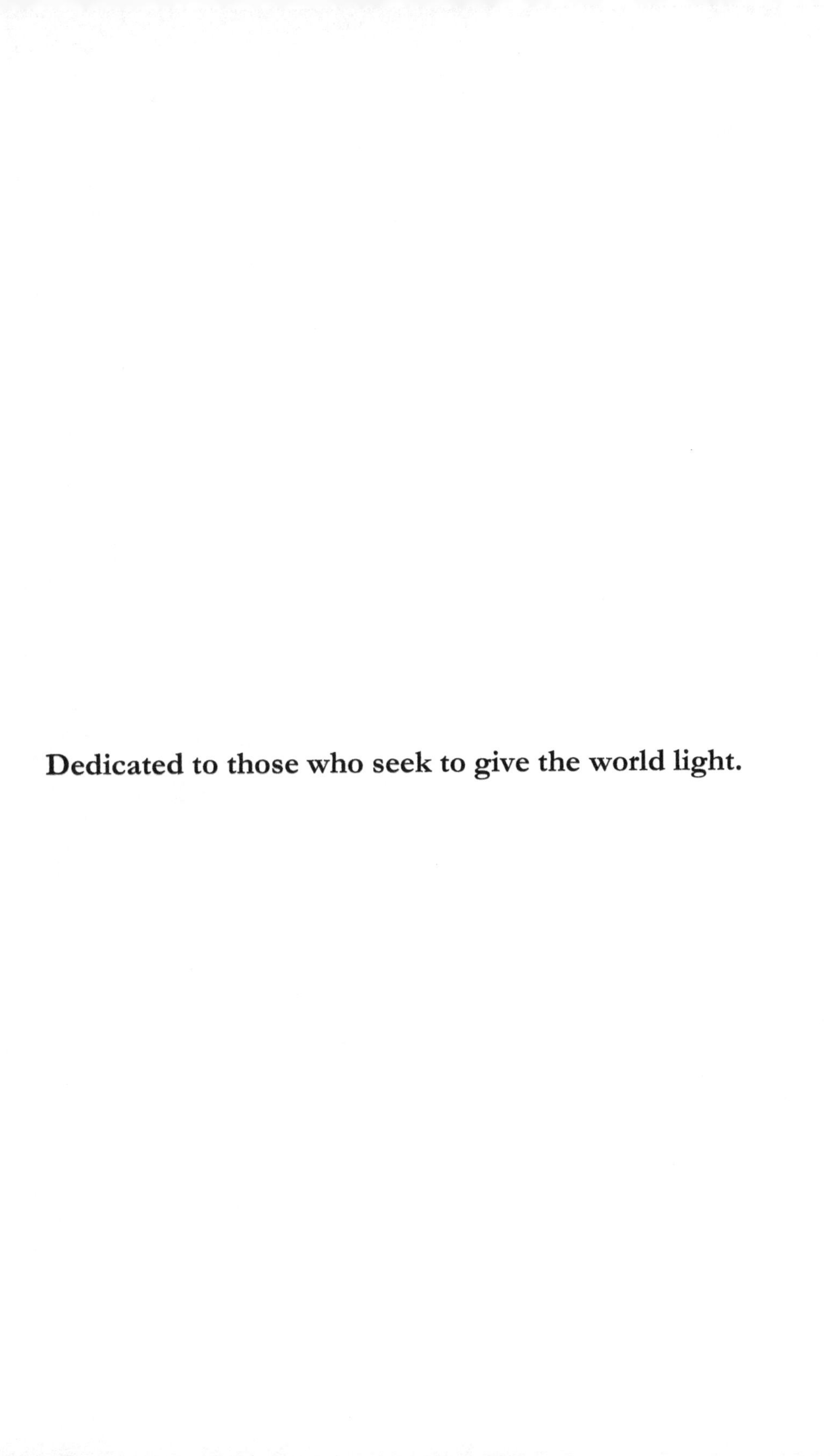

Dedicated to those who seek to give the world light.

"Between stimulus and response there is a space. In that space is our power to choose our response. In our response lies our growth and our freedom."

-Viktor E. Frankl

"As far as we can discern, the sole purpose of human existence is to kindle a light of meaning in the darkness of mere being."

-Carl Jung

Contents

Preface

I felt a strong, almost overwhelming drive to write this book which I attribute to both my professional and personal experiences. While working with patients coping with major depressive disorder, two of the most frequent questions I have received are "what am I going to do with the rest of my life", and "what is the point of living if I no longer have a purpose or a meaning to my existence". Answering these questions is no easy task as humans have grappled with these themes for many centuries.

Existential crises are extremely common, especially in patients with severe depression. This state of mind can be lonely, demoralizing, and spiritually draining. I often refer patients experiencing existential crises to study the writings of Dr. Viktor E. Frankl, a holocaust survivor, and the author of the timeless classic *Man's Search for Meaning*. The message of this book reminds us that meaning and spiritual growth are possible even in the bleakest and most challenging environmental situations. Dr. Frankl established logotherapy, a form of psychotherapy directed at helping individuals to find meaning and purpose in their lives. According to these principles, meaning can be found by working or creating, loving someone, and even adopting an alternative mindset in the midst of inevitable suffering.

I can empathize with these patients at a deeper level because I also experienced an existential crisis in my early 20's when the world felt as though it was spinning out of control and there was tremendous uncertainty pertaining to my future and my survival. I describe in detail how I reached that point in chapter 7 of the book. Through evidence-based treatments and the study of Dr. Frankl's teachings, I was able to overcome this despair, complete a doctoral program, and become a neuropsychologist. My greatest hope is to help as many people as possible to find purpose, with the aim of maximizing their potential and living life to the fullest. It is for this reason that I wrote *Pursuing Purpose,* which serves as a guide to understanding purpose and the critical role that is plays in our mental and physical well-being.

This book also describes strategies for determining one's own purpose(s) in life, presents daily lifestyle approaches for enhancing purpose and achieving a deeper spiritual satisfaction, and lastly, discusses cutting-edge neuropsychological interventions that can enable remission from depression and existential crisis.

Purpose is not easily found, but the pursuit of this elusive psychological construct is amongst the most worthwhile missions of our lives. I hope that the following chapters are beneficial to those of you that are on a mission to find your purpose. This book combines findings from psychology and neuroscience research along with the wisdom of Dr. Frankl to provide a comprehensive guide for pursuing purpose in modern times.

Chapter 1:

The Pursuit Begins

Close your eyes. Take a minute to imagine that one day you wake up and see the world through a new set of eyes. You are a living being, yet you occupy a shell that is in some ways familiar, yet strangely and eerily unfamiliar. You are floating undirected through an infinite array of clouds, colors, plants, and other living organisms that seem otherworldly or certainly out of the realm or your imaginative capacity. As you take in the sights, smells, sounds, and feelings from this novel external environment, your mind races through a repeated set of desolate questions: How did I end up here? What strange world am I occupying? Who am I in this bizarre place? What exactly is this existence? Bring your attention to how you may be feeling during this thought experiment: lost, lonely, melancholy, small, and possibly insignificant. Now, please open your eyes when you are ready.

The purpose of this short mental journey was to transport you into the headspace of a 22-year-old undergraduate student that was months away from graduating with a bachelor's degree in psychology from the University of North Carolina at Charlotte. This student was also a four-year player on the tennis team and was fortunate enough to have a sweet and beautiful girlfriend. The same student that on the outside appeared to have it all figured out and a well-paved, illuminated path to success was the same student floating hopelessly through a vast array of unknown. That very same student is now the author of this book.

Some contemporary psychologists have posited that the human mind is amongst the most powerful and resilient materials known to the universe that we inhabit. My personal hypothesis is that the human spirit can at the same time be as strong as a diamond or silicon carbide, but also more fragile than glass or the clinging jellyfish (Gonionemus vertens). Although it is very difficult to test this hypothesis empirically, there has been strong anecdotal evidence throughout the history of humankind. The human mind and spirit have contributed many wondrous creations to the world such as electricity, skyscrapers, jet planes, natural law, and of course the bacon cheeseburger, just to name a few.

The resilience of the spirit has also been on full display in individuals such as Joan of Arc, Galileo, Harriet Tubman, Socrates, Malala Yousafzai, and Viktor Frankl who overcame unimaginable obstacles and went on to become some of the most heroic humans in our history. Even on a daily basis, there are awe-inspiring acts achieved by everyday humans that may go unnoticed or unremembered in our history books but are nonetheless, sensational. Incredibly, that same human mind can unravel. Within just about any given circumstance, it can perceive despair, hopelessness, anxiety, and most demoralizing of all, a lack of existential purpose. If the human mind is a tool so powerful, and so impactful on our physical health, general well-being, and meaningful social relationships, then why is it that historically we have placed a minimal emphasis on managing mental health relative to physical health? If you are reading this book, you may be fascinated with the deep underpinnings of the human mind, and if you are like me, then this topic has captured your interest for as long as you can remember. Fortunately, since the birth of modern psychology in 1879 (Wilhelm Wundt in Germany) there has been an explosion in research aiming to explain phenomenon like consciousness, cognition, personality, behaviorism, neuroscience, and clinical disorders of the mind.

You may also be here to optimize your mind and maximize your potential to live a happy, successful, and purposeful life. Lastly, you may be someone that is feeling lost and purposeless, and seeking guidance in finding your own proper path in life. Regardless of the reasons you are here, I would like to welcome you and hope that you find this content valuable and applicable to your life and your own unique circumstances.

The following chapters contain topics and lessons that from my professional and personal insight will assist you greatly in the pursuit of your purpose. Purpose, according to Webster's dictionary, is defined as the reason for which something is done <u>or created</u> or for which something exists. I have underlined the phrase "or created" to highlight the human element of purpose. Regardless of one's religious orientation or their degree of faith we can all agree that human beings and other creatures were created by some extraordinary power or force. Since the beginning of human existence there has been a fascination with work, invention, and achievement. There is a strong reason that humans (well most) are simply not content with spending their days sprawled out on a couch or under a canopy with an umbrella drink and then rinsing and repeating. From an evolutionary psychological standpoint, many have argued that humans possess, at their very core, an innate drive to find their own, unique purpose.[1]

Purpose as a psychological construct is complex, and it is thus comprehendible why people spend many years and even decades of their lives trying to find it. Many people have sadly been unsuccessful in the pursuit of their own purpose. However, when a person finds themselves striving towards or executing that very thing that makes them feel completely present and gives them the impression that they are spending their time exactly the way that it should be spent, something beautiful happens. In that moment, a person is at the peak of their individual powers and becomes encapsulated in something which is of greater magnitude than their individual self.

There are four vital characteristics regarding purpose which are essential to its definition and ultimate manifestation in our lives. First and most important, purpose is entirely unique to the individual and can be vastly different between individuals or groups of people. For example, my core purpose in life from a young age has been helping others to navigate problems and overcome obstacles. However, another person's purpose may be to create a food dish that can magically bring a smile to all those who consume it. Second, purpose does not need to be singular; humans can have a multitude of purposes that may range from the general (abstract) to the highly specific

The Pursuit Begins

(concrete), and these multiple purposes exist in a psychological hierarchy of importance to the individual. For example, the general purpose of a teacher may be to educate and inspire many children; however, this same individual may find a greater additional purpose in caring for his or her family. At the same time, they may also find an important but far-less prioritized purpose of collecting themed-quarters for each of the 50 states in the U.S.

Possessing multiple purposes is an excellent strategy for softening the wounds caused by the failure or unexpected removal of a particular purpose, which will inevitably occur in life. For example, the teacher is one day promoted to a promising administrative role where interactions with students are significantly less frequent, or the artist experiences a tragic injury and can no longer produce beautiful paintings beloved by the world. These individuals can reinvent themselves and refocus energy on other purposes.

Further, purpose is adaptive and can fluctuate significantly throughout our lifespan. The purpose of a child may be to excel in sports or music, thus making their parents proud. That same child may hold onto that purpose to some degree but will likely take on new purposes with age such as playing a sport collegiately or professionally, and then eventually teaching that sport to their own child or other students of the game. Lastly, purposes are guided and driven by the cultural context within which a person resides. For example, an individual belonging to the Toto tribe of India (1377 people) may have more simplistic aspirations to feed their family and survive arduous living conditions. Should that individual be moved to the U.S. or another well-developed society, their goal may shift to making sure that their entire family's Christmas wish-list is fulfilled. Both culture and socioeconomic standing can exert a strong influence on one's purpose. If basic survival needs are comfortably met, then one is freely available to select more abstract purposes related to hobbies, leadership opportunities, and career goals.[2]

In summary, purpose is unique to the individual, is multifaceted, and is highly adaptive throughout our lives. One final characteristic of purpose is that when it is found we will be met with a degree of subconscious reinforcement. There is an element of "just knowing" when one has found or is working towards a purpose that is highly satisfying, fulfilling, and spiritually energizing. That being said, there are many objective means for tracking purpose gains over time which will be discussed later in this book. Finally, purpose is not easily found, but it can be easily lost, and it is for this reason that I wrote this book. I hope these pages will serve as a guideline to individuals that like me, have felt existentially lost but are always striving to achieve their own personal purpose in life.

Chapter 2:

The Essential Nature of Purpose

It is critical to note that purpose and meaning are words often used interchangeably, yet a fundamental difference by definition is that meaning refers to what is meant or conveyed by an action, word, or concept, while purpose is the precise reason for doing something. In the *Path to a Meaningful Purpose: Psychological Foundations of Logoteleogy*, Luis. A Marrero provides further useful distinction using the Greek origins of these words; logos (meaning) and telos (purpose).[3] Logos is best conceptualized with words such as reason, cause, ground, and expectation, while telos is encapsulated by words including closure, results, reaching, and consummation. It seems that meaning can best be explained by how something or someone is defined (one's intention) and purpose is the fulfillment or consummation of the meaning. Thus, it could be argued that purpose (applying meaning into action) is as essential if not more important than meaning for achieving psychological and spiritual enlightenment.

The Essential Nature of Purpose

Meaning and purpose have been the focus of a countless number of novels and empirical research studies, typically pertaining to fields of philosophy, psychology, and evolutionary biology. In his 1998 novel *The search for meaning in Evolutionary Perspective and its Clinical Applications*, Erik Klinger proposes that the search for meaning and purpose is rooted deeply in biology to the extent that goal striving is a biological imperative of all zoological organisms.[4] However, for the typical animal (including mammalian species) these goals are formulated with the aim of obtaining primary reinforcements (food and sex), which are imperative for both short-term and reproductive survival. Klinger goes on to conclude that humans have a similar biological drive, but our capacity for complex cognition and social goals is what elevates our biological drive towards the aim of achieving a higher-level meaning and purpose.

Adding to this compelling point, I believe that humans can only freely pursue these higher-level goals if primary reinforcers (food, shelter, social contact) are comfortably obtained throughout their lives. According to the World Health Organization (WHO), roughly 89 percent of the world's households were food secure throughout 2020. This type of security (although far from perfect) has enabled many modern humans to seek out higher-order purposes compared to previous eras of history.

One might suspect that humankind's enhanced capability for complex cognition would be reflected in biology through a comparison of the total brain mass and volume amongst species. However, with regard to average brain weight the human brain ranks behind other species including the sperm whale, elephant, gray whale, and even bottle-nosed dolphin. The culprit for enhanced human cognition is actually the expansion of the cerebral cortex, in particular the prefrontal area, relative to the rest of the brain volume.[5] The human cerebral cortex comprises 77 percent of the overall volume of the brain compared to a mere 31 percent in the rat brain, and an estimated 45 percent in our closest genetic relative, the macaque monkey. The complexity of the evolved human cerebral cortex is also evident in an investigation of the neurons or nerve cells within this area; on average, humans possess 16.3 billion neurons, while gorillas have 9.1 billion and elephants have 5.6 billion.[5]

Our increased cerebral cortex and prefrontal development has fueled and supported our boosted propensity to solve complex problems, form multidimensional social relationships, and strive for a higher-level of thinking and consciousness.[6] This advancement is both a blessing and a privilege, as it has allowed our species to produce unfathomable creations of beauty in domains of art, poetry, and literature, as well as machines that can incredibly mimic the work of a god. However, as alluded to in the classic tale of Adam and Eve, sometimes ignorance can be bliss. Our increased cognition and higher level of thought capacity have made us all too capable of questioning the abundance of unknowns that are inherently a part of the human experience and inhabiting planet earth.

For as long as we as a species have held the capacity to document our inner thoughts with pen and paper, humans have been searching for a purpose; either within the universe itself or at a more interpersonal level, within their respective nation, family, friendship, or romantic relationship. The seeking of such a purpose can be seen as a highly adaptive psychological response to the process of coping with fears of the great unknowns of the universe. It is also possible and has been suggested that humans possess a deeper, innate drive to find a purpose in order to live a successful and contributive life. Essentially, to feel that their time on earth was well-spent when it does reach a conclusion.

The constructs of meaning and purpose were classically and eloquently explored in Dr. Viktor Frankl's 1946 novel *Man's Search for Meaning,* a work that he wrote after surviving three years in a Nazi concentration camp. During this time, he tragically lost his mother, father, brother, and pregnant wife. A hallmark aim of the novel was to suggest that purpose can be found in even the bleakest and most horrific settings of the human experience, where life and spiritual growth seem utterly impossible. A reoccurring message is that "those who have a 'why' to live, can bear with almost any 'how'".[7] Frankl, a renowned neurologist and psychotherapist, even invented a therapeutic technique revolving around the psychological constructs of meaning and purpose, which he coined logotherapy.

Central to this theory is the idea that psychosis or psychological ailment is the direct result of a lack of meaning in one's life, and that an individual can dramatically improve their well-being by fully realizing their meaning and purpose. Similarly, a person who is skilled at maintaining optimism and finding purpose will possess an unaverred spirit even in the fiercest of environmental onslaughts aimed at that individual.

The core assumptions of logotherapy are that 1) life has meaning in all circumstances, even the most physically and emotionally exigent. 2)

The Essential Nature of Purpose

Our main motivation in living is our will to find meaning in life. 3) We each have the freedom to find meaning in our acts, experiences, or at least meaning in the stand taken, should we be faced with unchangeable suffering.[8] The positive outlook regarding one's circumstances that is fundamental to this theory has helped to fuel the development of positive psychology; an approach that strives for psychological healing rather than simply coping or managing psychopathological conditions and symptoms.[9] The beauty of this approach is that a sense of autonomy, power, and freedom is granted to the suffering individual in their recovery process.

To this day, elements of logotherapy (and positive psychology) are still commonly used in psychological intervention approaches for addiction, mood disorders, and existential crises. It is also an approach I frequently use when interacting with patients that struggle with feelings of shame and inadequacy following a psychiatric diagnosis.

When reviewing the results of a brain activation scan or clinical report, I feel it is necessary to emphasize not only the problematic traits but also the positive elements of a person's mind or brain functionality. For example, an individual coping with anxiety-related conditions will commonly present with heightened (fast-wave) activation in the right-central portion of the brain. This is a trait related to issues of over arousal including anxiety, insomnia, or ruminating; however, it is also found in individuals with high levels of conscientiousness, a personality trait related to diligence, grit, and strong work ethic. Individuals high in conscientiousness are often successful in their professional endeavors and can be some of the most genuine and caring people around.

The Essential Nature of Purpose

I try to elucidate to the patients that some of the underlying traits leading to their struggles may also be contributing to positive aspects of their personalities. The key to sound mental health is essentially maintaining a healthy balance. A societal shift towards a more accepting approach could further de-stigmatize mental health care, enabling countless individuals to access the care that will ultimately boost their well-being and quality of life.

It is important to note that the vast majority of people do not one day wake up and suddenly recognize exactly what their purpose in life is. Purpose is often fulfilled with great perseverance, and in many cases patience. Unbeknownst to most, Winston Churchill was actually exiled from England for controversial views and poor reputation in his 50's. However, he would go on to lead Britain as Prime Minister through World War 2 and play an instrumental role in the defeat of Hitler and Nazi Germany at the age of 66.

It was not until age 52 that Abraham Lincoln became president of the United States, led the abolishment of slavery, and prevented the division of the U.S. into two separate nations. J.R.R. Tolken (the famous author) was in fact 62-years-old when he wrote the timeless classic, *Lord of the Rings* in 1954. The great Samuel Langhorne Clemens, made famous by his pen name "Mark Twain", was 41 when he published the iconic and innovative novel *The Adventures of Tom Sawyer.*

At age 64 and in her 5th attempt, Diana Nyad became the first confirmed person to swim from Cuba to Florida without the aid of a shark cage. The 110-mile-long journey took her 53 hours straight. Sam Walton was relatively successful in retail management throughout his 20's and 30's, yet it was not until he was 44-years-old that he founded a little company known as Walmart in 1962 that would eventually be worth 429 billion dollars. Lastly, one of the most distinct and calming voices in the world belongs to Morgan Freeman, an actor that did not obtain his first starring role until age 49.

In summary, purpose and the closely related construct of meaning have long been fascinations and driving forces of the human experience. It seems that our enhanced propensity for advanced deductive reasoning has instilled within us a deep desire to live out and execute purposeful lives.[10] Pursuing purpose in life is a necessity for psychological and spiritual growth and those who are not content with their current existence or long for an alternative purpose will be at a significantly greater risk for psychological ailments and general issues of well-being. With the evolution of human cognition, we have also developed the ability to ask high-level and abstract existential questions about the universe, its creator, and whether there is a greater meaning behind it all. A major factor in achieving spiritual satisfaction is to feel that one's purpose has impacted not just the self, but also other humans (both proximal and distal), and that relevant contributions to the world may live on after a person is no longer living on earth.

The last part of the chapter highlighted a series of well-known individuals who after years of hard work and dedication were able to achieve tremendous success. The contributions of these individuals to the world are noteworthy and are inspiring examples of what can be achieved if one is to properly find their purpose. However, it is important to note that purpose and fame are by no means synonymous. There are countless everyday individuals who live incredibly purposeful lives and positively impact many others, but do not achieve widespread fame and recognition. Finding purpose is a rigorous but worthwhile task, often requiring many years of dedication, failure, and resurrection. Still, there are strategies that can assist in this existential pursuit and provide the best chance of succeeding and avoiding unnecessary psychological and spiritual strain. First, one must know where to start when it comes to recognizing and understanding their purpose.

Chapter 3

Discovering and Realizing Purpose

Given the multifaceted and fluid nature of this construct, one of the most challenging aspects of life is determining one's purpose(s). Admittedly, there are select individuals with prodigious abilities who establish purpose in their early ears. Examples of these individuals include Wolfgang Amadeus Mozart (composer), John Von Neumann (Mathematics), Judit Polgar (Chess), Sor Juana Inés de la Cruz (Literature), and Macauley Culkin (Kevin McCallister from home alone). At first glance, it is easy to feel envious towards these gifted individuals and their ability to find professional purpose as just children.

However, many child prodigies experience strong difficulties in other domains of life as they age, and eventually strive for updated and more timely purposes. For the rest of us non-prodigies, finding purpose is a task that may take months, years, and even decades to uncover. Still, there are certain strategies that will significantly increase the likelihood that purpose will eventually be found.

1.) Take note of what garners positive and negative feedback from those around you.

One of the key driving forces for these prodigies towards devoting the necessary time to their craft was the positive reinforcement they received from family, friends, and their teachers. Being attuned to the verbal and non-verbal reactions of the people around us can ultimately be very informative when it comes to discovering purpose. For example, Mozart received very early attention, encouragement, and praise from his father who was also his first teacher, and Judit Polgar's Scheveningen variation in the game of chess was met with not only rapid victory but also awe from opponents.

In my own childhood, friends and family members alike would frequently begin discussing various issues in their life with me. Following the conversation, these individuals often seemed less conflicted and sometimes even thanked me for listening. Once, a first-grade classmate confided in me that her mother was "being mean to her half the time and the other half not paying any attention to her". I still remember saying hello to this classmate every morning and wanting them to feel seen and attended to. Being able to help people work through mental and physical challenges has always given me a sense of deeper connection with the world around me and a sense that I was doing exactly what I should be in that moment. Helping others is a core purpose of mine and I have met a vast number of others who prioritize this common purpose. There are many cynics who scoff at individuals who find purpose in helping others, claiming their actions to be for self-interest only.

According to numerous sources, altruism or the motivational state or trait that a person possesses with the goal of increasing the welfare of another person is real and many individuals possess high levels of this construct.[11] Further, whether good deeds or charitable behaviors are truly of an altruistic nature is of minimal importance to the recipient of the generous action. It is true that helping others does provide many with positive feelings about themselves, but regardless of the motivation behind such deeds, it is difficult to argue that such behaviors do not make the world a better place to live. Other core purposes such as making people laugh, fixing wounds or illnesses, creating art, running faster than a greyhound, and even providing resources for one's family will often be discovered at an early age by the internalization of feedback provided to us by our friends, family, instructors, and even strangers.

2.) Talk, talk, look up from your smart phone and converse some more.

Rather than burying one's head in a smartphone (a device that has become the equivalent of an adult security blanket) every time one is out and about on their own, time would be better spent taking advantage of the knowledge accrued by the 7.753 billion people on earth (well many of them at least). This will be accomplished by conversing more with people, including the ones who live next door, the ones who go to your school, the ones who work at the coffee shops you are addicted to, and even the ones that supervise your work performance. Inevitably, some small talk can shift the conversation towards career talk. When approached with humility and politeness, nearly everyone is willing to share, some are even very eager to discuss their career accomplishments. Either way, conversing with others can lead to the discovery of career options that otherwise may not have been conceived, while also learning about the important factors (fulfillment, salary, hours, degree of difficulty) that may set apart good career options from poor ones.

Travelling home to South Florida from my freshman year of college in Charlotte, North Carolina I was coincidentally seated next to a gentleman who happened to be reading *The Lucifer Effect* by Philip Zimbardo (a terrific novel examining the social factors that contribute to genocide and authoritarian-led acts of individual violence). Subsequently, I asked him if he happened to work in the field of psychology. It turned out that he owned a successful therapeutic practice in the area and had even worked as a sports psychologist with the Miami Marlins baseball team for several years. Striking up a conversation with this individual allowed me to gain valuable knowledge about becoming a psychologist as well as some of the inevitable highs and lows of the job. This conversation ultimately cemented my interest in becoming a professional in the field.

3.) Discover your values by taking a standardized assessment.

Discovering and Realizing Purpose

According to psychologist and author Barbara Markway values are the principles that give our lives meaning and allow us to persevere through adversity.[12] In relation to purpose, understanding one's values may be an essential component to feeling as though they are on the proper path. There are endless examples of values including family, freedom, integrity, intelligence, creativity, faithfulness, morality, and spirituality, all of which impact our day-to-day behaviors and decision making. Gaining a keen understanding of our system of values can aid in the process of determining what purposes to attend to and strive for.

For example, if family is a fundamental purpose, then someone in their early 20's may want to forgo a single life with multiple shallow encounters for a deeper relationship with enough stability to begin a family. At the same time, a person in their early 20's placing greater value on adventure, freedom, and exploration may find themselves feeling trapped or confined in a traditional family environment, yet feel great fulfillment and satisfaction from frequent travel and a single romantic status. Additionally, a person with a core value of creativity is unlikely to find fulfillment in a career of law, data entry, and especially quality control, while a person placing high value on order may be just the opposite. Still, most people would accurately describe themselves as complex and multi-layered, making value determination a fairly difficult objective.

A great strategy for gaining a more fine-tuned understanding of one's core values is to select 5-10 key values from an extensive validated list. One such list that I highly recommend can be found in *The Confidence Gap,* a novel by Dr. Russ Harris, the author of numerous books about Acceptance and Commitment Therapy (ACT).[13] When I completed this exercise, I selected values in the following order; family, loyalty, selflessness, health/fitness, success, dependability, nature, love, gratitude, and spirituality. This core list will fluctuate with time to some degree but many of the values will endure throughout the lifetime. Becoming perceptive to such values can go a long way in helping one to conceptualize professional and personal purposes that will align with their core value system.

For those seeking a more comprehensive assessment of their values, there is an excellent online instrument called the "Life Values Inventory". The instrument was developed by R. Kelly Crace (Vice President for Health and Wellness at William and Mary) as well as Duane Brown (Professor Emeritus at the University of North Carolina- Chapel Hill). The program is highly convenient to use as a one-time tool for gaining insight into one's own system of values as well as for multiple uses, allowing one to track changes in this system over time. In step one, a series of value-related items such as "challenging myself to achieve", "improving my performance" "being accepted by others", and "protecting the environment" are listed and the user is to select how often a specific belief guides their behavior on a 1-5 continuous scale.

Step two involves clarifying the values from step 1 into categories depending on the importance that is placed on that value as well as how much attention is devoted to it. In the third and final step, the user selects the roles (work/academics, important relationships, and leisure/community activities) that they want to prioritize in expressing each value. The end result of this tool is a facilitated understanding of the critical values that a person holds, as well as the domains of life that they should be applied to.

4. Engage in frequent journaling to document your thoughts and examine patterns over time.

Reflective journaling has frequently been documented as a wonderful practice for sound mental health functioning.[14] Journaling provides a valuable opportunity for self-expression and gaining clarity on thoughts and feelings from earlier in the day. For many, this practice is of more benefit than actual talk therapy because of the full freedom for honest and uninterrupted streams of thought. Additionally, daily journaling has shown to enhance the functionality of the default mode network (DMN) of the brain which encompasses the posterior cingulate cortex, precuneus, medial frontal cortex, and inferior parietal cortex.

This activation network plays an important role in functions like emotional regulation, stress management and overall well-being.[15] Other trainings including yoga and mindfulness meditation can stimulate the default mode network and lead to improvements in conditions like anxiety, OCD, and PTSD. In the context of purpose, studying trends across daily journal entries can also give valuable context into the types of activities and interactions that are fulfilling and energizing, versus those that are draining and dogmatic.

Chapter 4:

Practices for Maximizing Purpose

Lofty Goals are Golden

As a child I thoroughly enjoyed reading books (along with an occasional video game), a sentiment shared by many across the globe. I was properly nicknamed by my third-grade teacher as the "window watcher" due to an affinity for spacing out into nature and engaging in daydreaming. Another contributing factor to this nickname came from my reading genre of choice at that age which was typically fantasy or fiction. Harry Potter, The Shadow Children, and the Baseball Card Series were a few of my favorites. However, of all the books that I read as a young child the one that shaped my personality development the most was *The Life You Imagine*, written by Derek Jeter, the legendary shortstop of the New York Yankees.

At the time, Jeter was the exemplary role model; a star athlete who was clean cut, supported charitable causes, and always averted the limelight enough to steer clear of the tabloids. One of the hallmark lessons of the book was the concept of "Setting Lofty Goals" from a young age. Jeter describes in detail the day that he "as a scrawny four-year-old child" marched into his parent's room and proudly professed that he would one day play shortstop for the New York Yankees, a dream that would incredibly come to fruition just 15 years later. To the credit of his parents, they did not laugh at this bold proclamation but replied that "you can be whatever you want in life as long as you work hard enough".[16] Reading about the idea that being a dreamer and setting lofty goals was not just a fantasy, was truly inspirational to me and probably encouraged a few more years of being the "window watcher".

On the topic of lofty goals, the great English author James Allen also wrote, "Dream lofty dreams, and as you dream, so you shall become. Your vision is the promise of what you shall one day be; your ideal is the prophecy of what you shall at last unveil." Setting lofty goals provides necessary inspiration to guide an individual to reach for the best version of themselves even in the mundane day-to-day experience, when immediate rewards are not always apparent. The power of a lofty goal is that it will raise the standard that one holds themselves accountable to, and ultimately help them reach their maximum potential. Whether it is becoming a best-selling artist, college athlete, store manager, or defeating an ailment or illness, we have the ability to drive many dreams into reality.

Maximizing Purpose

Paramount to this principle is the idea that true meaning and purpose are discovered in achievements of delayed gratification. As humans, we certainly have animalistic instincts that drive us towards the fulfillment of basic needs such as food, water, and sexual reproduction; however, the rapid development of the human prefrontal cortex has rendered us capable of advanced reasoning, planning and coordination, and emotional comprehension. This has spawned the pursuit of higher order goals like achievement, societal contribution, and legacy.

In his bestselling novel *The Happiness Hypothesis: Finding Modern Truth in Ancient Wisdom* renowned social psychologist Jonathan Haidt uses the metaphor of a wild elephant and the more rationale "rider of the elephant" to illustrate the two systems (rationale and instinctual) that exist within the human mind and brain. The elephant is strong and persistent in its drive to guide behavior towards instant gratification and drive reduction. However, when the elephant is successful and each of our basic needs and cravings are met, the result yields minimal satisfaction for the rider and the psychological well-being of the person. It is only when the rider remains in control that long-term lofty goals can be pursued properly, leading to greater purpose achievement.[17]

Two Marshmallows are Better Than One

In 1972, a group of 32 children (16 males, 16 females) in Stanford, California were volunteered by a parent to partake in an iconic study led by psychologists Walter Mishel and Ebbe B. Ebbesen in which they were offered a choice between one small but immediate reward, and two small rewards if the participant could successfully wait for a measured period of time. Little did these children know they were the first participants involved in the iconic "marshmallow test" and their ability to exhibit the

patience necessary for obtaining the larger delayed reward over a smaller immediate reward would aid in the development of the psychological construct known as "delay of gratification".

Follow-up studies conducted over the years would shed light on just how impactful this simple test would be in predicting future outcomes of mental and physical well-being. In a 1988 study, parents of the (now adolescent) participants from the original study rated those children who delayed gratification longer as significantly "more competent" in a variety of outcomes reflecting personal and academic standing.[18] In a 1990 study, the ability to delay gratification was strongly and positively correlated with SAT scores.[19] In follow-up studies, higher ability to delay gratification predicted other vital outcomes later in life including increased sense of self-worth, enhanced stress regulation, and lower likelihood to abuse illegal drugs.[20]

In 2011, a functional magnetic resonance imaging (fMRI) study was conducted on the original Stanford sample (now in their 40's at this time) to determine whether delay of gratification in preschool predicted functional brain differences in adulthood. Amazingly, the study revealed that children with high delays in the original study recruited greater prefrontal activation during a go-no/go paradigm (attention task involving button press to green arrow and suppressed response to red arrow) than the low delayers in the original study. At the same time, those who had low delay times 40 years ago, presented boosted activation in the ventral striatum relative to those with high delay times.[21] The ventral striatum is an area of the brain that sits in the center, just above and behind the ears. It is an important mediator of mood, learning, and addiction and is involved in signaling to us that something is rewarding and that we should seek more of it. Overactivation of the ventral striatum and corresponding under activation of the more reasonable and logical prefrontal cortex has been found to be a critical neurological mediator of addiction, motor tics, and thought disorders such as obsessive compulsive disorder.[22]

It may seem overly deterministic and a little concerning that a test conducted in preschool could have such a strong predictive influence on life outcomes such as academic achievement, emotional control, and life satisfaction. Fortunately, delay of gratification and the broader construct of inhibitory control (IC) can be improved directly through lifestyle habits as well as computerized training tasks. IC is one of the three key components of executive functioning (EF) ability along with working memory and mental flexibility.[23] EF refers to a critical set of abilities driven by the prefrontal cortex that are involved in decision making, solving problems, controlling impulses, and even marital success.

One of the Great Medical Curiosities of All Time

In the 1840's Phineas P. Gage of Grafton County, New Hampshire was working as a successful, good-natured, and hardworking railroad constructionist when a freak accident occurred that would forever change his life as well as well as modern psychology and neuroscience. On September 13, 1848, Gage was directing a work team assigned to blast rocks while preparing the roadbed for the Rutland and Burlington Road south of the village of Cavendish, Vermont.

Maximizing Purpose

The primary job of this crew was to clear rocks to level the ground, a task that involved placing an explosive charge deep into the rock by drilling a hole. The hole was then filled with gunpowder and a fuse was set; afterwards, sand was used to cover explosive material preventing direct contact. Lastly, a tamping rod was used to jam the explosives into the rock. As Gage was diligently working on this task around 4:30 p.m., his attention was momentarily distracted by his fellow coworkers behind him. Looking over his right shoulder, Gage inadvertently brought his head into line with the blast hole and tamping iron. He then opened his mouth to speak.

In the very instant Gage opened his mouth, the tamping iron began to spark against the rock and the powder subsequently exploded. Rocket-launching from the hole, the tamping iron which was 3.2 cm in diameter, 1.1 m long, and 13 pounds pierced through the left side of Gage's face in an upward direction, just anterior of the lower jaw. The rod propelled upward through the upper jaw, launching through the left side of the brain, then completely out of the top of the skull through the frontal bone.

The force of the blast was of such intensity that the rod ultimately landed 80 feet away from where it had initially struck Gage. Miraculously, Gage was able to walk on two feet within seconds and was speaking within minutes. Unfortunately, as he recovered from the injury in the coming weeks it became apparent that he (according to written accounts from his coworkers) "was no longer Gage". His coworkers further documented that "the equilibrium or balance, between his intellectual faculties and animal propensities, seems to have been destroyed. He is fitful, irreverent, indulging at times in the grossest profanity (which was not previously his custom), manifesting but little deference for his fellows, impatient of restraint or advice when it conflicts with his desires, at times pertinaciously obstinate, yet capricious and vacillating, devising many plans of future operations, which are no sooner arranged than they are abandoned in turn for others appearing more feasible".[24]

Due to his erratic and impulsive behavior, as well as his change in personality he could no longer work the railroad job and relocated to Chile where he worked as a stagecoach for several years. Eventually, he relocated to San Francisco, California where he died in 1860. This one-of-a-kind case study was the first notable demonstration of the remarkable ability of the brain to influence personality, impulse control, and rational decision making.

The left prefrontal cortex (where the rod exited) is now recognized as an especially critical brain area for the moderation of attention, mood, and energy. Some neuroscientists have even posited that this region of the brain plays a role in consciousness, or sense of self. The case of Phineas Gage exemplified the vital connection between brain and behavior as well as the concept of localization within the field of neuroscience. Brain localization is the advantageous practice of associating various physical and psychological functions with particular structures within the brain, using various imaging technologies.

The Evolution of Psychology and Neuroscience

Although this case signified the profound impact that brain health and functioning have on human thinking and behavior, for the next 100 years the field of psychology was largely dominated by two theoretical approaches: psychoanalysis and behaviorism.

Maximizing Purpose

Psychoanalysis was led by Sigmund Freud, Carl Jung, Alfred Adler, Karen Horney, and Melanie Klein, and placed a major emphasis on the role of the subconscious mind (thoughts, feelings, desires) in guiding our moods, behaviors, and mental well-being. Early behaviorism theories on the other hand proposed that human behaviors and emotions were guided entirely via environmental conditioning that was either classical (think Pavlov's dog experiment) or operant (increasing the likelihood of future behaviors using rewards and punishments) in nature. According to this viewpoint, which was led by John Watson, B.F. Skinner, and Edward Thorndike, the best approach to correcting psychological ailments was through ameliorating maladaptive behavior patterns.

Although these perspectives are extremely valuable to the field of psychology, they undervalue the important role that genetics and brain circuitry play in moderating behavior and cognition. This is ultimately problematic as recent studies have shown that many psychological phenomenon and clinical conditions have high heritability rates; 30-50 percent for personality traits, 57-73 percent for IQ, 36-96 percent for autism spectrum disorder, and 40-50 percent for major depressive disorder.[25]

In order to better stratify the role of genetics in manifesting mental health concerns, scientists look at patterns of illness in families to estimate their "heritability," or roughly what percentage of their cause is due to genes. The most common approach is to find people with the disease who have a twin, and then find out whether the twin also has this particular condition. Identical or monozygotic twins (think Fred and George Weasley) share 100% of their genes, while non-identical or dizygotic twins (think Mary-Kate and Ashley Olsen) share 50% of their genes.

If genes are part of the cause, we would anticipate a patient's identical twin to have a much higher risk of disease than a patient's non-identical twin. Another source of valuable information is the adoption study approach, which may explore whether an adopted person's risk of depression is greater if a biological parent also had depression. Results from both approaches have yielded a moderate-to-large size genetic link to depression. To be clear, there is not one specific "depression gene", "bipolar gene" or "autism gene" as is the case of certain diseases caused by a traceable genetic abnormality such as cystic fibrosis (mutation in cystic fibrosis transmembrane conductance regulator or CFTCR) or Huntington's Disease (caused by a single defect on chromosome 4).

Most mental health issues including depression and anxiety, (two of the most common ailments in the world) are caused by many clusters of inherited paternal and maternal genes. As a result, the study of epigenetics (how environmental contexts facilitate differential expression of genes) has shed light onto the pathways precipitating mental health concerns. Various environmental factors shown to increase the propensity of depressive symptoms include childhood trauma, obesity and other physical health issues, poor diets that are high in sugar, lack of exercise, impaired sleep quality, and lack of leisure time.[26] According to Viktor Frankl and other logotherapists, a perceived lack of purpose in one's given circumstances may also preface issues with depression and anxiety. If someone possesses a genetic susceptibility for depression, these factors will increase the likelihood for expression of those genes.[26]

The field of neuroscience has gained tremendous popularity in the last 60 years and has emerged as a vital bridge for making the field of psychology more scientifically and medically sound. First of all, medical tools for imaging the brain (magnetic resonance imaging or single photon emission computed tomography) as well as recording specific neurophysiological activation patterns (electroencephalogram or magnetoencephalography) have enabled the identification of measurable neural markers that signal risk for psychological or neurological conditions.

These objective measures can be highly advantageous for making diagnoses as well as determining whether a treatment has been effective or not. Additionally, the specific effect of genetic mutations can be studied on the brain, in humans as well as mice and chimpanzee models. In the case of complex conditions like autism spectrum disorder that have extremely broad phenotypes, this type of research will prove to be useful for pairing genetic abnormalities with specific neural markers and subsequent behavior changes. This may eventually lead to the development of customized medication or treatment options that will save families valuable time and financial burden.

The emergence of a sub-field known as cognitive neuroscience has helped to uncover the neural substrates of various mental processes. One construct called executive functioning (EF) has been given an immense amount of attention in this field because it seems to predict success in a myriad of different domains. Therefore, mastering EF abilities could be considered one of the keys to maximizing one's potential in life.

A Billion Dollar Brain Training Industry

According to the 2020 Global Market Report, the cognitive assessment & training market is expected to reach $11.4 Billion by 2026, rising at a market growth rate of 26.6%. A major driving force behind this movement is the aging population. Based on 2020 census data, there will be more than 46 million adults 65 or older living in the U.S. by year 2030. Roughly 1 in 5 Americans is projected to be 65 years or older by this time. Additionally, the explosion of the neuroscience field and relevant assessments of neurological functioning has led to a steep rise in public interest of this topic for the sake of maximizing brain health and cognitive productivity. At the heart of the brain training industry is the construct that was appropriately named executive functioning (EF).[27]

EF refers to a critical set of mental processes that are involved in selectively attending to environmental cues, responding appropriately, planning for future events, and regulating emotions in the pursuit of a desired goal. When covering the highly important topic of EF for one of my psychology courses I often introduce the topic by saying, "listen very closely class because this next topic we are discussing is important for just about every single facet of your life". EF has in fact been associated with academic achievement, job success, annual income, and even relationship and marital satisfaction. Today, the notion of executive functioning enhancement is a concept hitting the mainstream. Popular and heavily advertised computerized training companies such as Lumosity, CogMed, and Cognifit have millions of users that can access daily EF training regiments through their home computer, iPhone, or tablet.

Executive dysfunction (emotion and behavioral impairments resulting from frontal lobe injury or underactivation) is now considered a hallmark component of numerous neuropsychological conditions including ADHD, ASD, Alzheimer's disease, and Parkinson's disease. Additionally, evidence has emerged showing an association between executive functioning difficulties and many other conditions including major depressive disorder, bipolar type 1 disorder, OCD, and panic disorder. Much of this research has been generated using a cognitive assessment inventory from Cambridge Brain Sciences,[29] which I also use with clients to objectively track treatment-related improvements in cognitive abilities associated with depression, anxiety, ADHD, and OCD.

In year 2000, Akira Miyake and colleagues at Colorado University at Boulder assigned a sample of 137 college students to perform a large set of moderately challenging cognitive tasks that were frequently used to measure neuropsychological health. These tasks included the Wisconsin Card Sorting Test, Tower of Hanoi, Random Number Generation, Operation Span, and Dual Task Paradigm. Using a statistical technique called confirmatory factor analysis the authors searched for latent grouping factors with regards to performance on these tests. They were able to identify three unique, yet highly correlated components of "executive functioning" which were identified as inhibitory control, working memory, and mental flexibility. Over the years this three-factor conceptualization of executive functioning has garnered much support.

Inhibitory control is the ability to withhold an automatic thought, response, or action in favor of a more optimal but less automatic reaction. This skill is most commonly measured by a laboratory task called the go/no-go paradigm in which a participant is instructed to press a button when a desirable stimulus appears on screen (i.e. a green arrow) and to withhold a response when an undesirable stimulus appears (i.e. red arrow). In daily life, this skill is on full display when we are out with our friends the evening before a big presentation and instead of partaking in a festive round of shots we instead reach for a glass of water and get adequate sleep for delivering a successful presentation. Another example may occur when a boss or supervisor strolls over to our desk on a Friday afternoon to ask us if we can cover the Saturday morning shift. Instead of professing the 7 or 8 profanities that may immediately come to mind, we manage to pause a second and instead reply "yes sir, I would be happy too". Inhibitory control impairments have been identified in global conditions of cognitive decline such as Alzheimer's and Parkinson's disease, mood disorders including depression, anxiety, and OCD, as well as ADHD, addictions, and conduct disorders.[30]

Working memory (WM) is the ability to hold a set of information in mind and manipulate it; this skill is most commonly measured via a task called the reverse digit span in which a series of digits are displayed on screen in a certain order (i.e. 4, 7, 9, 2, 3) and the participant's job is to then type in the numbers in the reversed order (i.e. 3, 2, 9, 7, 4). Working memory is critical in our day-to-day life for remembering phone numbers, street addresses, directions, and the steps to solving complex problems at school and work. Working memory will also help a person to follow the details or series of events in a story they are being told, even if the story is very lengthy and a little redundant. The three subcomponents involved with this ability are the phonological loop (or the verbal working memory), visuospatial sketchpad (the visual-spatial working memory), and the central executive which involves the attentional control system.[31]

The reverse digit span captures the verbal working memory component and a task called the reverse corsi block can be used to assess visuospatial WM. Essentially, a series of blocks on a grid will light up in a fixed order and the participant is instructed to click on the blocks in the reverse order of what they witnessed occurring. Impairments in both visuospatial and verbal working memory are prominent in conditions related to global cognitive decline including Alzheimer's and Parkinson's disease as well as ADHD.[32] In ASD, impairments in working memory have been identified specifically in the verbal domain. Mood disorders (including depression and anxiety) have been associated with difficulties in both domains of WM, while minimal to no evidence has been found for WM deficits in bipolar disorder or OCD.[33]

Mental flexibility or task shifting involves the ability to actively shift attention between one task and another; this is most commonly measured using the Wisconsin Card Sort task. In this task, a number of stimulus cards are presented to the participant. The participant is told to match the cards, but not how to match; however, they are told whether a particular match is right or wrong. The purpose of the WCST task (includes 128 cards) is to classify cards, which differ by three criteria: color, shape, or number of the designs on the face of the cards, with the experimenter changing the criterion used after the participant makes 10 consecutive correct classifications. Thus, the objective is to determine how adept the user is at learning the pattern and effectively switching mental strategies for card sorting within the overall task. An example of cognitive shifting in every-day life goes as follows: A person wants to prepare a nice dinner for their romantic partner with massaman curry as the featured dish; unfortunately, while getting the ingredients ready this person realizes they have forgotten to purchase the curry powder. Shifting or mental flexibility would allow this person to find a suitable substitute for this dish like ground cumin. Shifting is impaired in global conditions of cognitive impairment, as well as autism spectrum disorder, OCD, depression, and bipolar disorder.[33]

Anyone that is interested in learning more about their own executive functioning abilities or would like to track their progress over time as a result of various trainings or lifestyle changes is advised to go to psytoolkit.com, a free-to-use cognitive testing site created and maintained by Dr. Gijsbert Stoet, a professor of psychology at the University of Essex. This resource includes 40 assessments capturing EF and other cognitive domains including WM, inhibitory control, mental flexibility, sustained attention, reaction time, and processing speed. It may also be advantageous to see a local neuropsychologist to complete a battery of supervised cognitive tests and receive both interpretation and recommendations from a professional. Many of these practices now also offer services that enable the mapping of particular brain regions, such as quantitative electroencephalogram (qEEG).

Maximizing Purpose

One question that is frequently asked about EF assessments is whether a person can take these tests daily for the purpose of stimulating their abilities. Unfortunately, taking these tests every day will lead to pronounced improvements on the tests themselves, however the transfer effects to other assessments measuring these skills will be minimal. This also means that this method of training will produce minimal benefits in regard to executive functioning that we would use

in a real-world context to help us meet our goals and live meaningful lives.

Notably, there is training that can be done in the home setting as well as some relatively basic lifestyle changes that can have a dramatic impact on our executive functioning ability. Regarding commercial software like Lumosity and Cogmed, there is mixed evidence to support the claims of these companies that daily training can facilitate substantial improvement in attention and working memory performance. Another website named Cognifit has been backed by randomized control trials (RCT); however, (similarly to Lumosity and Cogmed) additional research is still warranted. Two RCTs consisting of healthy elderly participants divided into an experimental condition (Cognifit training 3x per week, 20 minutes a day, 8 weeks) and a classic computer game control group (Tetris or checkers) found that the Cognifit group had significant gains in visual-spatial working memory, sustained attention, and focused attention relative to the control condition.[34]

An additional study found significant improvements resulting from Cognifit training on working memory (digit span) and broader executive functioning abilities (trail making test) relative to a control group that watched educational television.[35] These commercialized training platforms have numerous pros; they are convenient to use, not overly time demanding, and they have games that are described as tolerable and sometimes even fun to play. Unfortunately, the research to date does not elicit a tremendous amount of enthusiasm regarding the possible gains from these trainings.[36] In the realm of computerized cognitive training, one task has emerged as highly effective in facilitating executive functioning improvements as well as transfer effects to other domains of cognition. This tricky and demanding task is referred to as the dual-n-back, a variation of the classic n-back task generated by University of California Irvine professor Suzanna Jaegi in 2003.

The traditional version of the dual n-back task involves remembering a sequence of spoken letters and a sequence of positions of a square at the same time and identifying when a letter or position matches the one that appeared earlier. The task is adaptive in that as a user masters the first level (1-back) the difficulty will increase to a 2-back so that now the user will have to identify stimuli (spoken letter or positioning of the projected square) that are identical to the stimuli that appeared two trials before. If performance continues to improve the user will advance to a 3-back, 4-back, and so forth. In this regard, the working memory span of the user is constantly being flexed and exercised.

At the same time, cognitive flexibility (or shifting) is being tapped into because the task objective changes across the different levels and difficulties of the task. Lastly, the training is highly demanding of inhibitory control because it is necessary to remain continuously focused and avoid the dominant response which may be adhering to the rules of the 1-back format as one progresses to the more advanced 2-back level and beyond. Thus, the dual-n-back is a supercharged training of executive functioning ability, equivalent to high intensity interval training or HIIT for cardiovascular fitness and muscle strengthening.

A 2008 study published in the PNAS scientific journal established that the dual n-back led to do both improvements in working memory as well as fluid intelligence.[37] This finding is notable because fluid intelligence was previously thought to be impossible to train with computerized cognitive exercises. Fluid intelligence (*Gf*) refers to the ability to reason and to solve new problems independently of previously acquired knowledge. *Gf* is critical for a wide variety of cognitive tasks, and it is considered one of the most important factors in the potential for learning new material.

Since the original study, cognitive training programs revolving around the dual-n-back have yielded improvements in domains of cognition such as focused attention, visuospatial and verbal working memory, and mental flexibility.[38] Impressively, this training has also led to neurological changes such as increased white matter levels in the entire cortex with a left lateralization.[39] This finding was particularly significant in the corpus callosum (a bundle of fibers that connects both hemispheres and is involved with emotional intelligence). White matter is a reflection of myelin sheath, a substance of the brain that sort of works like an insulator, speeding up the rate at which a message from one neuron is transmitted to another. Higher volumes of white matter within the brain have been associated with improved cognition and reduced risk of cognitive decline and corresponding conditions of neurodegeneration.

In a recent study published in *Nature*, the dual n-back training group (16 sessions) showed improved memory performance that was accompanied by increased functional connectivity of the default mode network (DMN) in the right inferior frontal gyrus.[40] The single n-back training group did not show significant training-related changes. These results are notable as they show that a demanding short-term WM training intervention can facilitate major changes at the neurological level. The DMN contributes to memory consolidation, contemplating about the future, and neurological recovery.

The dual-n-back training is available for free download from http://brainworkshop.sourceforge.net/ and can also be accessed through https://brainscale.net/dual-n-back. For the best results, the training should be done at least 5 days a week and for a minimum of 20-30 minutes per day (for 40 sessions).

Emotional Executive Functioning Training

A more recent development in this field is the idea that emotional aspects of executive functioning are linked to emotional well-being and subsequently could hold an important key into a better understanding of mental health conditions like depression, anxiety, and OCD. For example, individuals with anxiety have shown longer response latencies on paradigms where one must inhibit response to an angry or fearful emotional expression. The attentional control theory (ACT) posits that anxiety increases the influence of stimulus-driven processing over top-down, goal-directed processes resulting in deficient attentional control, also referred to as inhibitory control. Additional research has shown that such inhibitory control impairments are driven by lower amplitude activation in frontal and central regions of the brain.[41]

Individuals with anxiety typically struggle to cope with a continuous flow of ruminative thoughts or worries that lead them to be more "inside of their own head" and less able to sustain focus to the environment around them. They may also be particularly distractible to stressful situations or those they perceive will evoke fear or frustration. By strengthening emotional aspects of executive functioning, many believe that individuals with anxiety-related conditions will have more strength and resilience in dealing with stressful situations, as well as more attentional control over distressing patterns of thoughts and emotions. Based on this premise, several research teams have implemented computerized training programs of emotional executive functioning. Thus far, these programs have yielded improvements in working memory and inhibitory control as well as reductions in anxiety or depressive symptoms.[42]

One of the leading innovators in this newer domain of psychiatry is Dr. Mark Ashton Smith and his colleagues at IQ Mindware. In addition to traditional cognitive training tasks featuring neutral stimuli, IQ Mindware has two training tasks aimed at improving psychological disorders of negative emotionality. The first is an emotional version of the dual-n-back which involves the presentation of two continuous stimuli; one is an emotional face (happy, sad, angry, scared, disgust, surprise, neutral) that appears in one of eight locations on screen and the other is an emotionally-charged word appearing in the middle of the screen written in different colors of ink (blue, green, red, pink, grey, yellow, gold, orange, purple). The task is not simple. A user must attend to the location that the face appears on screen and simultaneously attend to the color of ink that the word is written in. Thus, they are ignoring the emotionally charged cues (connotation of the word and emotionality of the facial expression) while they zone in on the task at hand.

Level one of the task involves pressing the "F" key when the location of the face is the same as the previous trial while simultaneously pressing the "L" key when the color of the word is the same as the previous trial. When a user performs 80 percent or better on level 1 they will move up to level 2, which involves pressing the keys when the location or color of the word matches what was shown from two previous trials before. The user will continue to move up levels and difficulties and thus, the training is adaptive. If this training sounds challenging you are not wrong, but it is challenging in the same way that a rigorous physical activity workout is. The brain is very much like a muscle in the body that needs to be stretched and exerted in order to be further developed or enhanced. I would argue that many people do not properly exercise their brains and as a result are not able to reach their full mental capacity and potential.

Given the degree of difficulty in the emotional dual-n-back, a less demanding training was developed that could help children (and less patient adults) to reap the benefits of emotional executive functioning training. This version is referred to as the emotional gFocus task and it involves the presentation of a continuous stream of blended stimuli, consisting of an emotional expression (male or female) projected in either an indoor or outdoor setting. These blended images are generated by altering pixel intensities through various weightings (default set at 50% face, 50% scene). In each training block, the participant is instructed to focus on one of four cues related to the images (male, female, indoor, outdoor) and in a "go/no-go" style procedure, they are to press the spacebar when the desired cue appears and withhold response when it does not appear.

Both of these trainings require merely 15-20 minutes a day and can be downloaded onto a home computer or tablet through the https://www.iqmindware.com/website. The emotional dual- n-back has been found to improve symptoms of anxiety and worry in college-aged students, PTSD in adolescents and adult veterans, and emotional regulation in adults with borderline personality disorder.[42,43] The emotional gFocus is a newer application but there has been some preliminary support for its utility.

Given the fascinating potential of emotional executive functioning training, I took the opportunity to study the emotional gFocus and its effects on preadolescent anxiety levels as well as resting-state brain activity patterns for my dissertation project. The study examined the relationship between anxiety, inhibitory control (IC), and resting-state electroencephalography (EEG) in a critical age-range for social and emotional development (8–12-year-olds). The participants were assigned to four weeks of either the emotional gFocus, a non-emotional version of the gFocus, or a waitlisted control condition, and were tested on cognitive, mood, and EEG measures.

The training was computerized and completed remotely for exactly 16 sessions. Overall, the emotional training condition showed improvements in IC accuracy, as well as reductions in anxiety compared to the waitlist condition. Additionally, brain activity in the lateral frontal region shifted leftward in the emotional training group. This is a neurophysiological change reflecting reduced risk for the development of an anxiety disorder.

These findings highlighted the promising potential of computerized IC training for mitigating negative emotional functioning in preadolescents. Short-duration computerized training is appealing, but it may not be the most suitable approach for many, and some might find it overly frustrating or even boring. Fortunately, yoga, mindfulness meditation, physical activity, sport training, and breathing exercises have also shown to positively impact executive functioning

Chapter 5

Lifestyle Strategies

The following practices for maximizing purpose may seem fairly intuitive but they can be life-changing if followed closely and executed with regularity and consistency:

1.) Boosting time management in day-to-day life.

The key benefit of improved time management is that more minutes of the day can be allocated to purposeful tasks and less time will be wasted. Better time management will be afforded by starting the day earlier, which entails waking up once the alarm clock begins buzzing as opposed to hitting the snooze button a dozen times and reaching back for the blanket.

Studies have illustrated that sleep inertia, the slow-crawling period between sleep-induced brain fog and full wakefulness can last anywhere from between two to four hours. If a person rolls out of bed at 8:30 a.m. to get to work at 9, there is a very high likelihood that they will not arrive ready to do their best work. Getting up early affords the body a chance to reach peak wakefulness naturally. This could be the difference between depending on just one cup of coffee as opposed to five espresso shots throughout the day, decreasing later feelings of anxiety and subsequent exhaustion. It will not be easy to start setting the alarm for an earlier hour, and it may entail a few days of strong resistance from your subconscious mind (or sleep-self) but once it becomes part of the routine, there will be a noticeable difference in energy levels and mental clarity in the morning.

That extra hour or two is also the time when a person can finally accomplish the hobbies or practices that lie at the top of their to-do-list, but sadly never actually make it off the list. These include lifting weights, training for a 5K or marathon, learning a new language, or engaging in yoga or morning meditation. In addition to feeling more awake during the day, these added practices will aid in the process of realizing the best version of the self. Other benefits to waking up earlier include reduced risk of depression for women over the age of 18.[45]

Additionally, in a survey study conducted with 367 university students, biologist Christoph Randler found that what they say is true, "the early bird really does get the worm". He found that earlier risers tend to get better grades in school, which get them into better colleges, which then lead to better job opportunities. He also concluded that morning people are better problem solvers and decision makers, two vital components of executive functioning ability.[46] Lastly, evidence has emerged that night owls are more likely to develop sleep disorders, sleep less overall, and wake up feeling more stress about their daily obligations.[47] Overall, sleeping 7-8 hours is very important and waking up an hour earlier than a person currently does could be the ticket to a more successful life.

Going along with the goal of improved time management, time spent on social media applications "or the new digital drug" should occur in moderation. I suppose the one exception would be if one's identified purpose is to become a successful social media promoter or influencer but even this should probably be secondary to other goals in life. For better or for worse, social media has become as automatic of a process as turning on the television or checking emails. In 2019, it was reported that nearly 4.6 billion people use at least one form of social media on a regular basis with the average individual having a whopping 8 social media accounts.

The award-winning Netflix documentary: "The Social Dilemma" presented some eye-opening and bone-chilling trends that have been identified in the social media age. First, the documentary identified that people with social media accounts are referred to as "users". In other industries it is commonplace to refer to people as "participants" or "members". The term "users" is common to one other industry, and that is the drug industry. This term evokes imagery of addiction, dependence, and potential withdrawal and this is exactly what social media engineers are aiming for.

Therefore, these companies are staffed with experts on attention, attraction, and human psychology who write algorithms that will present and guide a person with the content that has been deemed most interesting and appealing to them. The goal is to obtain more and more users that get increasingly addicted to the content that is fed to them on a continuous loop by their social media app.

The second point made is that social media was not made with morals, it was made with the key purpose of profit. As a result, fake news that is not backed by credible sources or science is shared rampantly and opportunities for cyber bullying or trolling are all too easy given the anonymity of the app as well as the perceived safety of knowing that a real-life confrontation will not occur following an online battle of insults. Google and YouTube engineers are very well-versed in the cognitive psychology concept of confirmation basis, first introduced by Tversky and Kahneman in 1974. This concept posits that humans will prefer and be much more comfortable with information that fits with their current opinions or worldviews, especially on controversial topics such as politics and religion. The algorithm decides what we will view, which means different users will get different results for the same search. These systems are built to feed our headspace the results and perspectives that fit into our preexisting cognitive schemas. Unfortunately, this process can foster intolerance of other perspectives.

In contrast, the path to growth, understanding, and toleration of other people and other perspectives involves the Piagetian process of accommodation, or adjusting our preexisting schemas or beliefs based on the absorption of new information. There is also a high risk that the information we are being presented through these modalities is not rooted in factual information or based on well-validated research.

I would go as far as to say that this process of information shielding (via Google and YouTube) has contributed greatly to the current dissonance in the United States. In an insightful analysis from Northwestern University Professor James Druckman (and colleagues) that utilized nationally representative survey data from 1970 to 2020, the authors calculated the difference between Americans citizens' positive feelings toward their fellow partisans and their negative feelings toward the opposing parties. On average, the feelings toward fellow partisans have remained consistently warm, yet feelings toward *opposing* parties have regressed from "apathetic" to downright "icy".

Those negative feelings have swelled to such a degree that they have now surpassed warm feelings toward fellow partisans, manifesting out-party hate into the popular feeling in American politics.[48] Research is also emerging to show that people are less inhibited and more hostile when they communicate online;[49] a phenomenon that further spreads the distance between in-group and out-group ideology and leads to the alienation of individuals.

The third point is that social media apps are rewiring the dopaminergic systems in our brain, leading to the depletion of natural dopamine levels in the presence of species-typical experiences like meeting friends for dinner, playing pickleball, or spending time at the beach or hiking mountains. Instead, when engaged with social media for hours a day and a continuous stream of personalized, attention-grabbing content, dopamine production is rampant.

According to Anna Lembke (Chief of the Stanford Addiction Medicine Dual Diagnosis Clinic at Stanford University) this flood of dopamine related to social media content leaves us in a state of dopamine-deficit when we step away from the phone or tablet.

Lifestyle Strategies

It has gotten to the point that we experience mental and physical anguish when we finally step away from the dopamine activating content in the form of "getting likes and comments", "viewing attractive people and places", and "watching content related to topics that we are enamored by".[50] A major issue with frequent social media use is the potential for addiction and the impedance of fulfillment in day-to-day life.

New York University Professor Adam Alter has equivocated the sensation of getting a like on social media to taking a stimulant drug like Adderall or Ritalin. Because of this tremendous reward, people curate their image on Instagram and Facebook, showing only their shining romantic moments, most prestigious accomplishments, and lavish trips to places like Bora Bora. After all, social media is the place to promote the best version of oneself. Unfortunately, there is a subconscious process by which people will compare their day-to-day realistic life (which may consist of breakups, scoldings from their boss, and financial hardships) with the unrealistic social media life of their friends or favorite celebrities (which often consist of bottle service at night clubs, new cars, and major economic victories).

Neuroscientific research (using fMRI) has shown that a jealousy network of the brain comprising the medial prefrontal cortex and ventral striatum is activated while a person engages in these social media "social comparisons".[51] In contrast to the psychological angst generated by social comparisons, a healthier approach is comparing one's lifestyle situations to prior renditions of their own self; thus, striving for attainable personal improvement rather than living like Kim Kardashian, Beyoncé, Leo DiCaprio, or Drake.

The fourth point is that we have been entered into the largest sociology experiment ever conducted, without our provided informed consent. Our data is constantly being used for marketing and advertising purposes. Just as we are fed video content that appeals to us, we are constantly being shown advertisements for clothing, food, and cologne that we are going to have a very difficult time ignoring. We are seen as part of a global experiment where apps compete for our attention and our privacy is sold to create a future where one day we could be manipulated or controlled by artificial intelligence.

There are obvious benefits to social media use including the ability to communicate with friends and family across the globe, sharing and receiving useful information, and being provided with instant entertainment (looking at you cat videos). However, it is important to be aware of some of the dangers of social media and like anything else, limit use to a reasonable amount.

2.) Moving the body on a frequent basis.

An estimated 40% of people aged 65 and older experience some degree of age-related cognitive decline. In the U.S., that corresponds to approximately 21 million people. Whether a person is 65 or older and trying to delay or reverse natural, age-related memory loss or if they are younger and simply looking to maximize cognition and performance, research overwhelmingly shows that exercise is one of the most important habits to implement. In addition to causing enhanced activation of the dorsolateral prefrontal cortex (executive focus center of the brain) physical activity promotes neurogenesis or the process of growing new neurons as well as synaptogenesis, which is the forming of new synapses or connections amongst neurons.

The key moderating factor is that exercise leads to increased production of neurotrophins, which are proteins that act as growth factors within our central and peripheral nervous systems. As we age, the volume of our brains naturally decrease, due to the reduction in size of individual brain cells and the number of connections between them reflected in grey matter and white matter, respectively. These reductions contribute to gradual decline in cognitive functioning over time.

One of the key neurotrophins involved with protecting against cognitive decline is brain derived neurotrophic factor (BDNF). BDNF has been popularly nicknamed as "fertilizer for the brain" because of its ability to aid in the regrowth of neurons and synapses, even when cells have been damaged as a result of chronic stress, traumatic brain injury, or age-related decline.

Recently, James Mortimer and Yaakov Stern conducted a 20-year longitudinal study with 454 older adults that agreed to donate their brains for research when they passed away. The participants were given accelerometers, a device to track their movements and physical activity every second of every day. There was a positive correlation between steps and hours spent in moderate physical activity (anything that lifted heart rate above average) with memory and speed of processing performance. Each one standard deviation increase in moderate physical activity hours was associated with a whopping 31% lower risk of dementia and corresponding decreases in white matter in the brain.[52]

Lifestyle Strategies

In another recent study, 160 elderly people with mild cognitive impairment were assigned to one of four conditions: aerobic exercise 3x a week for 45 minutes, eating a heart-healthy, dietary approaches to stop hypertension (DASH) diet, combining aerobic exercise with the DASH diet, or receiving health education. Following the six-month intervention, the researchers evaluated the executive functioning abilities of the participants. While the DASH only condition showed no improvement and the educational condition showed reduced capacity, the exercise group presented significant improvements and the DASH + exercise had the best outcomes.[53]

These results have been mirrored in young adults as well; a study from Sanna Stroth and colleagues implemented a jogging intervention for 30 minutes, three times per week for 6 weeks. Following the intervention, the authors found significant pre-to-post improvements in positive emotional affect as well as visuospatial working memory.[54] In another investigation, participants aged 20-67 were randomly assigned to a 6-month, 4 times weekly program of either aerobic exercise or stretching/toning. In the aerobic condition, a plethora of positive outcomes occurred. BMI was reduced, executive functioning was improved, and cortical thickness was increased in the left frontal cortex.[55]

Since the benefits are apparent and irrefutable, the question becomes how much exercise and what types are most helpful for improving brain health? The American College of Sports Medicine recommends a minimum of 150 minutes of moderate aerobic exercise per week along with resistance training at least twice per weak. This might include the use of dumbbells but could also feature resistance bands and bodyweight exercise such as pushups, pull-ups, squats, and planks.

An ideal workout week may consist of 3-4 days of moderate-to-rigorous (70-85 percent of maximum heart rate) aerobic exercise (walking, jogging, biking, rowing, swimming, elliptical, dancing), 2-4 days of resistance training (depending on goals), and 1 day a week of rest.

The most important part is sticking with a plan that enables consistency. The majority of physical activity intervention studies to date have shown that a minimum of 6 months of training is necessary for inducing stable cognitive changes.

A promising trend for healthy young adults is the use of High Intensity Interval Training or HIIT, sometimes referred to as circuit training. The hallmark feature of HIIT is continuous and rigorous bouts of work (sprints, rope jumps, mountain climbers) interspersed with relatively brief periods of recovery. When the body is at peak exertion during HIIT, it relies on anaerobic pathways (breaking down glucose without oxygen) to provide necessary energy for completing the exercise.

This process creates instant but limited energy, which means the length of time that max effort can be sustained is very short. If HIIT is done properly the intervals should only be about 20 seconds, with adequate recovery time. This will usually equate to a 2:1 or 3:1 ratio of rest-to-work. For example, if someone was engaged in 20-second sprints, they should rest for 40 seconds to one minute before beginning the next intense interval. On a rate of perceived exertion scale (RPE), HIIT should evoke between a 7 and 10. Many young adults are favoring this form of workout because not only is it challenging and adventurous, but it is also significantly less time consuming than moderate aerobic workouts. Additionally, research is beginning to uncover powerful effects from this type of training.

A 2021 investigation on 67 adults that were in COVID-19 lockdown assigned participants into either a HIIT condition or moderate-intensity training (MIT). The two groups (HIIT and MIT) were assigned the same exercise volume consisting of 40-minute sessions (6 days per week), over the course of 6 weeks. Depression, anxiety, stress, and resilience were assessed before and after the intervention. Notably, both conditions had reduced stress levels, as well as symptoms of anxiety and depression, however the results were significantly intensified in the HIIT condition.[56]

Team sport training is also a highly beneficial means for achieving a physical activity workout. Activities like tennis, basketball, soccer, football, volleyball, and hockey enhance social cooperation, ability to collaborate with others, and resilience to handling inevitable defeats and losses in life. Additionally, there is some newer evidence showing that long-time team members actually have neural synchronization when they complete a task together. Specifically, one study found that 12 dyads of individuals on the same basketball teams had significantly greater neural synchronization in the lateral prefrontal area during the completion of a joint drawing task compared to 12 dyads of college classmates. This finding demonstrates that the synchronization of behaviors often observed amongst teammates extends to the domain of neurophysiology as well.[57]Based on this result, Michael Jordan and Scottie Pippen likely had strong neural synchronization.

3. Fueling the body with the right nutrients to feel great and make gains.

"Let food be thy medicine, thy medicine shall be thy food." – Hippocrates.

It is worth noting that many of the nutrients obtained in foods are precursors to neurotransmitters (NT) and the number of precursors consumed has a direct influence on NT levels within the gut and brain.

Foods do not actually contain neurotransmitters but the right diet with proper amino acids and healthy proteins can have a positive impact on neurotransmitter levels. Neurotransmitters function as the body's chemical messengers. They are the molecules used by the nervous system to transmit messages between neurons, or from neurons to muscles. Notably, electrical energy bursts in the neurons, often referred to as action potentials cause the release of neurotransmitters. Neurotransmitters influence automatic nervous system responses like breathing and heart rate, but they also influence psychological functions such as learning, emotional affect, fear, pleasure, and happiness.

Two of the vital and widely discussed neurotransmitters in the brain are dopamine and serotonin, although there have been approximately 100 discovered to date. While dopamine is typically labeled as the "pleasure chemical," this is a misnomer given that a flood of dopamine in the brain does not actually induce waves of pleasure. However, dopamine does connect sensations of pleasure to certain behaviors or imagery (e.g., dopamine flood while watching Guy Fieri visit the world's greatest hamburger shop or Pioneer Women preparing key lime pie bars), thereby reinforcing feelings of pleasure.

The old saying, "you can have too much of a good thing" certainly applies to the dopaminergic system. Too much consumption of food, alcohol, sex, pornography, video games, or phone-use can lead to dependence on these substances or activities for dopamine production, leaving a person feeling fatigued, anxious, or irritable when they are deprived for certain periods of time. This also diminishes the dopamine response to traditionally prioritized human activities including socializing with friends, going on dates, and spending time in nature.

Dopamine is made in the brain through a two-step process. First, the amino acid tyrosine is converted into another amino acid called L-dopa, and then this amino acid is metamorphosed into dopamine. Although it is unrealistic to pinpoint single causes of mental health and neurocognitive issues, many conditions including Parkinson's disease, ADHD, Schizophrenia, depression, and addictions have been linked to dopamine irregularities in different parts of the brain.[58]

In schizophrenia, the most supported theory is that the presence of too many dopaminergic receptors in the mesolimbic pathway results in hyperactive limbic systems, leading to positive symptoms of schizophrenia such as hallucinations, delusions, and illogical thoughts. Other research points to the possibility of hypoactivation (and deficient dopamine levels) within the prefrontal cortex. This finding could explain the onset of negative symptoms of schizophrenia including difficulties with attention, decision making, and logical reasoning.

It has been confirmed that Parkinson's disease mainly results from low or depleting levels of dopamine due to the damage or death of dopaminergic neurons in the substantia nigra, a critical part of the basal ganglia for initiating smooth and coordinated movements.[59] Research has confirmed that dopamine levels in ADHD are also irregular, likely due to excessive amounts of Dopamine Active Transporter, a transmembrane protein that carries dopamine away from the synaptic cleft so that it is no longer usable.

In terms of depression and dopamine, a direct link has not been established; however, depleting dopamine levels may necessitate attentional and motivation concerns that are common in depression. Lastly, the misuse of drugs such as cocaine can preface a rapid spike of dopamine in the brain, leading to a dependence on the substance to achieve production of dopamine.

In recent years, scientists have discovered that the gut and brain are so closely linked that the gut is sometimes referred to as the "second brain". The gut contains a large number of nerve cells that produce many neurotransmitter-signaling molecules, including dopamine. As far as impacting dopamine levels by consuming foods that are rich in L-tyrosine and L-dopa, the ideal strategy is to follow a diet that is high in protein like beef, chicken, eggs, milk, and cheese as well as omega-3 rich fish such as salmon and mackerel. Dark chocolate, nuts, and avocados have also proven to be advantageous.

Personally, I find the taste of beets to be pretty repulsive, but they are a terrific source of L-dopa if they can be consumed. Steering clear from foods with high levels of saturated fats is also helpful. One study on rats found that those consuming 50% of their calories from saturated fat had reduced dopamine signaling in the reward areas of their brain compared to animals receiving the same amount of calories from unsaturated fat.[60]

Velvet beans, also known as *Mucuna pruriens*, naturally contain high levels of L-dopa and there is some direct evidence to support a beneficial effect of this food on dopamine levels in the brain. One study testing individuals with Parkinson's disease found that the consumption of 250 grams of cooked velvet beans significantly raised dopamine levels and reduced Parkinson's symptoms one to two hours after the meal. Additional studies on the effects of *Mucuna pruriens* found that eating this food is even more effective and longer lasting than traditional Parkinson's medications with the added benefit of fewer side effects.[61]

Notably, velvet beans are not yet FDA approved for the treatment of Parkinson's and as usual "you can have too much of a good thing". Cooked velvet beans and powder supplements can be toxic in high amounts. Because of this, it is recommended that a person consult with their doctor before taking this supplement to rule out contraindications. Several other vitamins and minerals are necessary for creating dopamine and if the body is deficient in one or more of these nutrients, it may have trouble generating proper dopamine levels to meet the body's needs.

These include iron, niacin, folate and vitamin B6. Deficiencies in any of these nutrients can be detected via blood work, and subsequent supplementation can be used to address dopamine deficiencies.

Another substance shown to improve attention, memory, and reaction time in young adults is docosahexaenoic acid (DHA) from fish oils.

The other omega-3 fatty acid in fish oil, eicosapentaenoic acid (EPA), has seldom been linked to cognitive benefits but it has been shown to reduce depression levels. Taking approximately 1 gram per day of DHA has been shown to be highly beneficial for battling neurocognitive decline. Although caffeine can provoke anxiety and does possess many drug-like qualities, it has proven to aid in memory and sustained attention, as well as buffer against conditions of cognitive decline like Alzheimer's and Parkinson's disease.[62] Caffeine can of course be obtained through tea, dark chocolate, and everyone's favorite cup of joe (coffee).

Acetyl-L-Carnitine is a natural amino acid produced by the body and has similarly shown performance enhancement benefits in young adults (reaction speed, sustained attention) and cognitive protection for elderly populations when a 500 mg dose is taken. Ginkgo biloba is an herbal supplement derived from the *Ginkgo biloba* tree which also happens to be one of the world's oldest living tree species, dating back to the ancient times of 350 million years ago.

Although it is unlikely that users of this supplement will absorb up to 350 million years of wisdom, this product (when taken at 60 mg, 2x per day) has shown to improve sustained focus and working memory by boosting blood flow to the prefrontal cortex.[63] Lastly, Bacopa Monieri (300 mg per day) and Rhodeola Rhosea (300-400 mg) have shown to improve thinking skills, mental alertness, and memory, as well as buffering age-related cognitive decline.[64]

Lifestyle Strategies

Serotonin is a key neurotransmitter involved in mood stabilization, feelings of well-being, happiness, sleeping, eating, and digestion, just to name a few functions. Deficiencies in serotonin levels have been associated with the presence of depression, anxiety, and insomnia, as well as increased susceptibility for these conditions. Serotonin is made from the essential amino acid L-tryptophan (by way of conversion to 5-hydroxytryptophan or 5-HTP). It is optimal for this amino acid to enter the body and be synthesized for the brain by way of food consumption. The most common foods containing high levels of L-tryptophan are nuts, cheese, and red meat. Ten additional foods that are high in L-tryptophan which ultimately boost serotonin levels are salmon, spinach, pumpkin seeds, sweet potatoes, almonds, cacoa and anchovies. Perhaps the eccentric and (slightly odd) person in your family that orders anchovies on their pizza actually knows exactly what they are doing. Unsurprisingly, L-tryptophan can be more efficiently translated into the neurotransmitter serotonin if adequate sleep, exercise, and sunlight are obtained.

One more point of emphasis is that a healthy amount of carbohydrates are needed for L-tryptophan to be converted into dopamine. Healthy carbs include quinoa, taro, buckwheat, yogurt, sweet potato, and brown rice. Lastly, it is a common myth that tryptophan consumed in food (e.g., turkey during thanksgiving) leads to excessive drowsiness or instant couch rest following the meal. I would urge people concerned by this to do a little Thanksgiving Day science experiment next year where they only eat the Turkey and pass on stuffing, sweet potato, apple pie, and wine.

Lifestyle Strategies

It is likely that they will not feel nearly as exhausted and that the copious amounts of food consumed on Thanksgiving are the real culprit rather than spiked L-tryptophan levels from turkey. In reality, turkey, chicken, and beef contain approximately equivalent levels of L-tryptophan (about 350 mg per 115 g), while other foods high in protein (pork or cheese) contain more L-tryptophan per gram than turkey.

One investigation of the utility of a high L-tryptophan diet (consuming Talbinah) for improving mood and positive affect yielded positive effects in a sample of young adults in Malaysia.[65] In another large survey study,[66] annual L-tryptophan consumption via food was negatively correlated with depression and positively correlated with social cognition, measured using the reading the mind through the eyes test. Participants were asked for information on their general consumption of L-tryptophan-rich foods via a checklist where they had to answer on an ordinal scale how often they consumed each item (not at all, several times a year, about once per month, several times a month, several times a week, daily, several times daily).

Despite these encouraging findings, further research is certainly necessary, and some researchers are skeptical that plasma L-tryptophan levels can be altered through diet changes alone. Sixty mg of L-tryptophan can also be taken to increase levels if dietary changes are not feasible. In a recent meta-analysis of 11 randomized controlled studies, it was found that L-tryptophan intake led to significant improvements in depression and anxiety, however trait aggression was not impacted. The authors concluded that 140 to 3,000 mg was the effective dosing depending on weight.[67]

Lifestyle Strategies

4. Providing nourishment to the spiritual self.

The notion that religion and spirituality are among the featured cultural factors that provide structure and meaning to behaviors and value systems is accepted in disciplines of theology and science. In a 2001 meta-analysis, researchers at the renowned Mayo Clinic concluded that spirituality and religious involvement relate to better long-term physical health and longer lifespans, lower rates of depression, anxiety, and suicide, as well as higher quality of life even in the presence of terminal illness. Lastly, evidence shows that spiritual fulfillment can play an important role in recovery from physical and mental illness.[68]According to a recent Gallup poll, in the past two decades the percentage of Americans who do not identify with any religion has nearly tripled (8% in 2000 to 13% in 2010 to 21% in 2021).

In year 2021, 47 percent of the U.S. population reported attending a place of religious worship with regularity compared to 70 percent just 20 years ago.[69] A potential explanation for the concerning decline of religious worship is a disconnection between the modern generation and certain religious laws including practicing sexual abstinence until matrimony as well as mandatory opposite-sex marriage. Additionally, rising global divorce rates have led to a disengagement in traditional family functions like attending religious ceremonies as well as eating dinner together on a nightly basis.

I possess a strong appreciation for many of the moral values taught by structured religions as well as the enhanced opportunity for community and social connectedness that is enabled by many of these institutions, however I do not entirely agree with the all-or-nothing approach that is required in many of these faiths. If one simultaneously developed appreciation of the moral guidelines and traditions of the Hebrew Torah, the elements of forgiveness and inclusion of Christianity, and principles of enlightenment and meditation from Buddhism, I believe they should be welcomed to practice their customized form of religion freely.

The opportunity for independent thinking and value selection within the context of traditional religions could lead to increased accessibility and appeal for modern generations. In my opinion, faith and spirituality should primarily help guide an individual towards forming a meaningful and comforting relationship with God, thus promoting strength, conviction, and acts of love while simultaneously preventing existential fear. Traditions are certainly of value but some degree of adaptation to modern times and dilemmas is necessary.

Given the many benefits of religion and spirituality on mental and physical health, it is unfortunate that more and more individuals are turning away from religious observation in modern times. Hopefully, these individuals are finding alternative means for feeling faithful and connecting to a higher spiritual power. A recent Pew Research Center survey found that approximately a quarter of adults living in the U.S. (27%) now identify as "spiritual but not religious", up 8 percentage points from 2017.

This trend is consistent across both males and females, as well as different age-ranges and ethnic groups.[70] Alternative expressions of spirituality may include self-directed prayer, meditation, singing, journaling, and philosophical practice. Regardless of the outlet that is selected, faith and spirituality are critical elements in the pursuit of purpose. In the wise words of famed American singer Mahalia Jackson, "Faith and prayer are the vitamins of the soul; man cannot live in health without them".

Stoicism: From Marcus Aurelius to Modern Times

Many sociological ecosystems of western culture have evolved to a point where death and mortality are seldom themes at the forefront of our consciousness, and it is even more seldom for one to encounter death on a regular basic unless they serve in professions like an ER nurse or medical examiner. This is intriguing as from a historical perspective, people had far shorter lifespans, illnesses were more prominent, and emergency medical care was less accessible. Individuals may have been frequently reminded of their own mortality by witnessing others in the village pass away on a near daily basis, as opposed to getting mere glimpses of it as they flip on Netflix and watch popular violent series like Mind Hunter and Ozark.

Still, wise individuals may go through their life appreciating their own mortality and understanding that the sanest and most logical philosophy is to find a purpose, maximize their productivity and creations, and hopefully experience many enjoyable and meaningful times along the way.

A group of philosophers whose slogan is memento mori (death on earth is inevitable) and whose bible is the book *Meditations* authored by the great roman empire Marcus Aurelias, refer to themselves as stoics. A common misconception is that stoics are not permitted to show any emotion or have normal human reactions. This is quite misleading as a stoic is actually a person who learns to distinguish between circumstances in life that they have control over versus those that they do not.

This allows a stoic to devote maximum focus and effort towards the tasks that they can control while mitigating their time spent worrying or in a perpetual state of anxiety. One fundamental goal of a stoic is to appreciate the grand scheme of the universe and to recognize that despite our best efforts to forget this inconvenient truth, we are all mortals. As a result, it is important to contemplate and even meditate daily on mortality and a life well-lived. Stoics hold the mindset that this type of meditation will leave an individual with a desire to take action, be virtuous every day, lead by example, focus on what can be controlled, and that ego and feelings of entitlement should be diminished. Other stoic principles include the idea that we are all equally valuable as human beings and therefore, no one should live with selfishness or spend their days seeking out hedonistic pleasures.

In line with principles of logotherapy, stoics promote a life of acceptance and maintaining composure and character even in the most exigent of circumstances. The writings of Marcus Aurelius and Lucius Annaeus Seneca (another famous roman stoic) teach us that the ultimate goal for a human is to one day reflect on the life that was lived with fondness and to know that the best possible effort was put forward consistently. Additionally, it is vital that an individual remains stable and consistent in their goals and mentality, and that they set a proper example for the significant people in their lives. In many ways it is a righteous approach to living life, and there are many positive parallels that can be drawn between stoics and devout religious individuals. However, individuals who are stoics do not necessarily align with an organized religion but instead strive to live virtuous and exemplary lives because they are in pursuit of a higher-order purpose that is only obtainable if the big picture questions of life are contemplated on a regular basis.

At any rate, part of a purpose-filled life should be pondering mortality and contemplating how current actions impact future renditions of the self. In modern times, stoicism is alive and well, thanks in part to bestselling author Ryan Holliday who has now written five novels containing themes of stoicism including *The Obstacle is the Way*, *Ego is the Enemy*, *The Daily Stoic*, *Stillness is the Key*, and *Lives of the Stoics*.

The Obstacle is the Way reached #1 on the Wall Street Journal Bestseller list in 2019 and has been frequently used by Miami Heat head coach Eric Spoelstra to motivate players on the team including Chris Bosh, who cited it as his all-time favorite novel. Following an on-field spinal injury that left him unable to walk, former Pittsburgh Steelers linebacker Ryan Shazier credited *The Obstacle is the Way* for helping him to overcome an onslaught of mental setbacks and ultimately heal his mental state and spirit. Over 300,000 people around the world (including myself) also subscribe to "The daily stoic", a newsletter presenting a daily meditative exercise of stoicism.[71]

Chapter 6:

Measuring Purpose in Life

"Without proper self-evaluation, failure is inevitable" – John Wooden

In determining whether one has been successful in their pursuit of purpose or whether they are traveling on the optimal path, there are many objective approaches for tracking improvements over time. However, it is worth noting that consistently following the suggested lifestyle changes in the previous chapter will likely be intrinsically rewarding on its own due to activation of self-efficacy and self-discipline. In the field of neuropsychology, to monitor changes over time practitioners rely most heavily on three different forms of measurements. These include self-reported or observer-rated questionnaires, cognitive performance assessments, as well as neuroimaging or neurophysiological instruments. In clinical practice, we may simultaneously use a Hamilton Depression Rating Scale Questionnaire, a digit span test of working memory ability, and a quantitative EEG recording to evaluate the progression of a patient as a function of treatment.

When determining whether an individual is on the right path in terms of pursuing their purpose there are numerous self-report questionnaires that can accomplish this goal. There is also emerging research in the field of neuroscience that certain resting-state and functional activation traits of the brain may correspond to higher levels of purpose. This research will be discussed later in the chapter, and hopefully objective neuroimaging tools will continue to be used with greater prevalence in the future.

Questionnaires Designed to Capture Purpose

Over the years, several assessments have been created to evaluate one's scores on the construct of purpose. One such inventory "The life Engagement Test" (LET) was devised by Micael Scheier and colleagues at the University of Carnegie Mellon in 2006. The LET consists of just 6-items and is designed to measure purpose in life, defined in terms of the extent to which a person is engaging in activities that are personally valued.

This was one of the first created scales to measure whether a person is currently experiencing purpose in life in the very moment of the assessment, rather than whether their entire lifespan has been filled with purpose. The LET consists of six items, three items framed in a positive direction (items 2, 4, and 6) and three items framed in a negative direction (items 1, 3, and 5). The following instructions are used for completing the scale. "Please answer the following questions about yourself by indicating the extent of your agreement using the following: 1 = strongly disagree; 2 = disagree; 3 = neutral; 4 = agree; 5

Measuring Purpose

= strongly agree. Be as honest as you can throughout and try not to let your response to one question influence your response to other questions. There are no right or wrong answers."

The items of the scale are as follows: 1) There is not enough purpose in my life, 2) To me, the things I do are all worthwhile, 3) Most of what I do seems trivial and unimportant to me, 4) I value my activities a lot 5) I don't care very much about the things I do, and 6) I have lots of reasons for living.[72]

The data suggests that the Life Engagement Test (LET) is psychometrically sound across different gender, age, and ethnic groups and is appropriate for widespread use. Interestingly, in the original research study on this assessment the authors also recorded data relating to important elements of psychological and physical well-being and correlated these factors with LET scores in participants from eight different samples. These included 1) a community-based sample of younger adults (n = 193), 2) female osteoarthritis patients (n = 183), 3) male spouses of osteoarthritis patients (n = 168), 4) a community-based sample of middle-aged women (n = 378), 5) women with early stage breast cancer (n = 198), 6) women with late stage breast cancer (n = 86), 7) a large sample of undergraduate students (n = 359) and 8) an even larger sample of undergraduate students (n = 511).

The outcome measures included optimism, self-mastery, self-esteem, emotional stability, physical health, marital adjustment, and life satisfaction. The LET scores were correlated with each of these outcomes in the study. For interpretation, small correlations span from .00 to .30, medium correlations range from .30 to .50, and large are characterized by .50 and higher. The LET scores were strongly and positively correlated with optimism in all eight samples that were surveyed (correlations ranging from .39 to .61). The same was true for both self-mastery and self-esteem scores in all samples except for 7 and 8 (which were not tested on these outcomes). The correlations were significant and ranged from .43 to .61 indicating moderate to strong relationships. With regards to emotional stability, correlations were significant in all samples (ranging from .34 to .48). LET outcome scores were also positively correlated with physical health scores in samples 5, 6, and 7 (ranging from .24 to .31) as well as both marital adjustment (ranging from .25 to .48) and satisfaction with life (ranging .34 to .51) in samples 1 through 7.

In terms of clinical symptomology, purpose scores were significantly and negatively associated with depression scores (using the Center for Epidemiological Studies Depression Scale) in samples 1 through 6, indicating that as purpose scores increase, depression scores are significantly decreased. The same finding was also true for depressive and anxiety symptomology using the Brief Symptom Inventory (BSI) in samples 7 and 8.

Based on this original study it is safe to conclude that the Life Engagement Test is a vital outcome measure given its significant positive correlations with self-esteem and optimism and negative correlations with symptoms of depression and anxiety. The life engagement test was also utilized in a large population-level study where results demonstrated a strong positive association between average life engagement score and a countries' Gross Domestic Product (GDP).[73]

Measuring Purpose

This suggests that purpose levels are increased as a function of economic productivity and opportunity. Additionally, the LET was studied in relation to the Internet Addiction Test (IAT) to determine the influence of internet addiction on reported purpose. In line with prior research on internet addiction and addictions in general, individuals with higher levels of dependence were left feeling more out of control of their actions and emotions and subsequently, their purpose in life.[74] The perception that one has control over their life outcomes is known as an internal locus of control. Holding this mindset has proven to have a positive impact on well-being, self-esteem, and relational attachments. In contrast, an external locus of control represents the belief that one is purely driven by their circumstances, this links to a higher potential for psychological issues.

Purpose in Life Test

To better assess the critical construct of purpose as outlined by Viktor Frankl's principles of logotherapy, James Crumbaugh and Leanard Maholick created the purpose in life test (PIL) in 1964. The instrument includes 20 items and participants are instructed to circle the number (1 to 7) that is most personally applicable for each statement. A user can add all the numbers (totaling between 20 and 100) and a score of < 50 is used to denote "an existential void" where an individual is feeling a lack of meaning or purpose in their life.

The validation study surveyed a sample of 225 subjects divided into 5 subpopulations. Group 1 comprised of 30 working-adult, non-patients while group 2 comprised of 75 undergraduate college student, non-patients. Group 3 included 49 outpatients of various cooperating psychiatrists in private practice in the state of Georgia and Group 4 consisted of 50 outpatients of the Bradley Center, Inc. (a privately endowed nonprofit outpatient psychiatric clinic) with mixed diagnoses. Group 5 consisted of 21 hospitalized patients, all with alcoholism.

There was significantly accurate distinguishment between patients and non-patients, and a progressive decline in mean scores from Group I through Group V, both for the total scores and for most of the individual items of the PIL. Being a patient was related to a steeper drop in the scores of males than for females. The instrument proved to accurately classify between patients and non-patients with 65.4% for females and 75.4% for males.

PIL scores were also not related to a subject's age, suggesting that purpose is an impactful construct for all ages. The Minnesota Multiphasic Personality Inventory was also analyzed in relation to the PIL and of the 10 subscales (hypochondriasis, depression, hysteria, psychopathic deviate, masculinity/feminity, paranoia, psychathernia, schizophrenia, hypomania, social introversion) depression scores showed the most meaningful relationship to the PIL (correlation of .30).[75]

Numerous studies have illustrated the PIL's effectiveness in predicting levels of occupational meaningfulness, degree of engagement in college campus activities, and life expectancy among prison inmates. Elsewhere, higher PIL scores were associated with lower anxiety levels and increased self-confidence and self-acceptance.[76] Higher PIL scorers are also more likely to experience heightened life satisfaction, perceive more positive expectations for their future and possess boosted emotional stability. When the Eysenck Personality Inventory was combined with the PIL, the researchers found that individuals with higher PIL scores are also less neurotic and more extroverted and open to experience.[77]

More recently, purpose has inspired fascination in other domains of psychology including stress management, addiction, and self-control. In a hallmark investigation, it was found that the perception of purposelessness in life mediated the relation between excessive stress and substance abuse.[78] The same researchers later found that sense of purpose was linked to an individual's level of depression and that a lack of purpose related to greater likelihood of drug use among women and suicidal ideation among men. Further, studies have shown that purpose predicts responsibility and self-control.

In 2006, William Molasso and colleagues sought to determine the types of activities and hobbies that are impactful on purpose for college-aged students. Factors that were significantly and positively related to purpose in life included more time spent exercising, studying, attending parties or social events, attending educational workshops, talking with professors, and discussing current events with friends. Interestingly, time spent watching TV and playing video games was significantly and negatively related to purpose in life.

It is not surprising that behaviors which promote both social engagement (i.e., attending parties or having discussions with friends) as well as goal achievement (i.e.., studying or exercising) are positively impactful on purpose while leisurely behaviors that are not socially salient or challenging would leave participants feeling a little bit empty and purposeless. This work is intriguing as it suggests that by way of choosing our activities and hobbies, we can have an active influence on our sense of purpose. The most encouraging takeaway from this study is that partying in college leads to higher levels of purpose[79] In summary, both the LET and the PIL are well-validated instruments for assessing levels of purpose in our lives. In terms of gaining a comprehensive review of one's purpose pertaining to clinical conditions, the PIL test may be more suitable; however, in order to take a short duration, more fluid checklist to measure one's purpose, the LET is more desirable and less time demanding.

A Purposeful Day and Positive Mindset Keep the Doctor Away

Given the link between the psychological construct of purpose and a myriad of physical and mental health outcomes, it is advantageous to determine how purpose relates to health markers that are assessed using heart rate variability, cholesterol, BMI, Electroencephalogram (EEG), and Functional Magnetic Resonance Imaging (fMRI). If purpose is correlated to these outcomes, then it may be possible to reduce risk of heart attack, rapid aging, stroke, and even Alzheimer's disease should purpose be obtained or enhanced in some way

It has been widely established that an important mind-body axis connection does exist in humans and other organisms. In support of this notion, there has been a fascinating line of recent research from Dr. Alia Crum (professor at Stanford University) and colleagues. Overall, the research demonstrates that "stress mindset" or one's classification of stress as either an exciting challenge or a detrimental threat to existence plays a critical mediating role as to whether stress will ultimately lead to positive or negative health outcomes.

Mindset research has proven useful for understanding how mentality affects survival pertaining to terminal illnesses, physical activity effectiveness, and even likelihood to succeed as a Navy SEAL.

Measuring Purpose

A 2020 study on the "stress mindset" of cancer patients showed that positive stress mindset or viewing the diagnosis as a manageable challenge rather than a catastrophe was related to lower levels of depression and anxiety as well as higher survival rates.[80] In a 2019 study on oral immunotherapy for the treatment of food allergies, patients that held a mindset that unpleasant body reactions to the micro amounts of allergen were signs that the treatment was working rather than weakening the body, had a significantly greater likelihood of successfully completing the treatment.[81]

Additionally, after studying 174 navy seal candidates, Crum and colleagues found that even in such an extreme setting, the stress-is-enhancing mindset predicted increased persistence within training exercises, speedier obstacle course times, and more positive evaluations from both peers and instructors.[82]

A 2007 study from Alia Crum and Ellen Langer tested whether or not hotel room attendants would burn more calories if they thought of their work as exercise rather than a job. For the experimental condition, the researchers met with the room attendants, explained that they were interested in better understanding physical fitness in the workplace and proceeded to present information about the caloric expenditures associated with different aspects of their work. They explained that changing sheets and towels for 15 minutes burns approximately 40 calories for the average 140-pound women.

Also, for a woman with the same weight, vacuuming for 15 minutes burns up to 60 calories. They closed by explaining that in an eight-hour workday these women could be burning as many as 1900 calories. In the control condition, they only explained the studies interest in workplace fitness, however they did not disclose the specific information about how their work is in a way "like exercise". In both conditions they recorded blood pressure, height, weight, body fat percentage and waist-to-hip ratio at the start of the study and then one month later. Only in the experimental group did weight, percentage of body fat and blood pressure all significantly drop, all thanks to a change in mindset about obligations in the workplace.[83]

This line of work has also extended to the realm of nutrition. In a 2011 study from Crum and colleagues, all participants consumed the same 380-calorie milkshake; however, half of them believed it was an indulgent, 620-calorie milkshake while the other half believed it to be a healthier, 140-calorie milkshake. The indulgent participants actually reported feeling more full following milkshake consumption and amazingly showed lower blood levels of ghrelin (a hormone produced by the gastrointestinal tract often labeled as the "hunger hormone"). Together, these studies show the powerful effects of mindset on meaningful biomarkers of physical health in addition to perceptions of mental well-being.[84]

Implications for Alzheimer's Disease

Dementia commonly affects elderly people (most often 65 years and up), but it is more severe than species-typical cognitive decline due to aging. Dementia occurs when brain cells, or neurons, are damaged and no longer network properly. Different types of dementia are characterized by how and where the cell damage occurs. The most common form of dementia, Alzheimer's disease, accounts for 60 to 80 percent of cases, and has been the focus of many purpose in life investigations.

Measuring Purpose

Although numerous neuroanatomical targets are affected in Alzheimer's, one of the most impacted areas is the hippocampus, a seahorse-shaped region of the brain associated with short-term and long-term memory. Through mechanisms still being elucidated, proteins called "beta-amyloid" and "tau" accumulate in neurons, leading to neurofibrillary tangles and subsequent cell death and improper functioning of broad circuits within the brain.

The disrupted cell-signaling in Alzheimer's disease primarily manifests as memory loss, starting with recent events and then generalizing into more episodic or personal experiences. Alzheimer's has major health and public policy implications as the baby boomer generation is now aging and Alzheimer's already affects 44 million people in the world. By 2050, the number of people aged 65 and older with Alzheimer's disease may grow to a projected 78 million, barring the development of medical breakthroughs to prevent, slow, or cure this devastating disease.

Thus far, the effectiveness of various medications including Aricept, Execlon, Razady (cholinesterase inhibitors), Memantine (glutamate modulator), and Aducanumab (beta-amyloid plaque redactor) has been mixed; with most studies showing moderate and short-term improvements at best.

The FDA's decision to approve Aducanumab has been in question, particularly due to their close-knit ties to Biogen, the company that manufactures the drug, as well as the relatively unconvincing evidence for the effectiveness of the drug in the two major clinical trials conducted thus far. Hopefully, in the near future a more impactful medication will be discovered. Unsurprisingly, this line of research is receiving enormous amounts of funding and scientific attention. Recent work by Patricia Boyle and colleagues at the Rush Alzheimer's Disease Center has found that purpose in life (PIL) could be one factor that contributes to neuroprotection (brain-preservation) against cognitive decline. In one study, the researchers monitored approximately nine hundred older adults at risk for dementia over a span of seven years and found that those with a high PIL (average score of 4.2) were only 50% as likely to develop Alzheimer's disease as those individuals classified as low PIL (average score of 3.0).[85]

This finding occurred even after the researchers controlled for other factors that could contribute to Alzheimer's risk like demographics, depressive symptoms, personality vulnerabilities, social network size, and number of chronic medical conditions. Those scoring high on PIL were also 30 percent less likely to develop mild cognitive impairment, a condition characterized by minor cognitive deficits that could (but doesn't always) progress to Alzheimer's.

In another investigation, the researchers examined the relationship between PIL and cognitive change over time in individuals already diagnosed with Alzheimer's. For the study participants, a higher sense of purpose was associated with slower rates of cognitive decline.[86]

Utilizing MRI technology, higher purpose has also been related to fewer macroscopic infarcts (lesions in both cortical and subcortical regions) signifying less neurodegredation in elderly adults as a function of increased purpose in life.[86] Additionally, the research team studied the autopsy specimens of individuals diagnosed with Alzheimer's and specifically looked at the amount of beta-amyloid and tau deposits in their brains. Individuals who had a high PIL before death scored higher on cognitive functioning, even when they did show higher clustering of Alzheimer's-related proteins. Lastly, in a five-year investigation of 1,238 elderly people without dementia, higher purpose in life was strongly associated with a lower risk of mortality during that time frame.[87] In summary, the innovative work of Patricia Boyle and colleagues has established high levels of purpose as a proven buffer against negative outcomes related to aging including cognitive decline, severity of Alzheimer's symptoms, and even mortality.

Purpose and Risk of Stroke/Cardiac Arrest

Neither the brain nor the rest of the body can operate properly without the heart delivering a reliable and consistent supply of oxygen-rich blood. The success of this delivery depends heavily on vascular health. When blood vessels fail to oxygenate brain tissue due to hemorrhage or obstruction, a stroke will occur. Across the lifespan, strokes are the fifth leading cause of death in the United States and when they do not result in death, they can precipitate major speech, motor, and cognitive disabilities.

Both healthy dieting and moderate to intense physical activity are effective means for mitigating stroke risk. Additional research suggests that having a high sense of purpose may also play a role in prevention and prognosis. Eric Kim and his colleagues at the University of British Columbia assessed the predictive influence of PIL on stroke risk in approximately seven thousand older adults who had never had a stroke. The researchers tracked the participants over a four-year period and found that for each standard deviation increase in PIL score, the adults reduced their stroke risk by roughly 22 percent.[88] The result occurred even with the researchers statistically accounting for

Measuring Purpose

behavioral, biological, psychological, and socio-demographic influences that could have confounded or interfered with the result.

Similarly, Kim and colleagues tracked 1,500 individuals with cardiovascular disease for two years and found that a higher baseline PIL was associated with a significantly lower risk of heart attack. Specifically, for every 1-point increase on the baseline PIL (on a seven-point scale) there was a 27 percent decreased risk of experiencing a heart attack over the course of the two-year study. In another large-scale study on adult males, the association between PIL and cerebrovascular-related mortality was measured over the course of 13 years. The authors found that a strong sense of purpose was associated with a 72-percent lower rate of death from stroke, a 44-percent lower rate of death from cardiovascular disease, and a 48-percent lower rate of death from any cause.[89]

Two potential mediators of the association between increased purpose and lower risk of both cognitive decline and stroke are inflammation and depression levels. Inflammation and depression are commonly implicated in ailments that afflict the central nervous system and respiratory system, including multiple sclerosis, Alzheimer's, Parkinson's, fatty liver disease, diabetes, rheumatoid arthritis, cancer, and obesity.

Inflammation is triggered by our immune systems which are made up of cytokines (peptides that influence other cells) that allow for communication between immune cells. Inflammation is adaptive both for clearing infection and healing bodily wounds; however, excessive inflammation leads to damaged cells throughout our various systems, and subsequent disease.

Measuring Purpose

In the case of depression, there are often deep-rooted and chronically high levels of psychosocial stress. Our body's response to stress is mediated by the hypothalamus-pituitary-adrenal (HPA) axis in which psychosocial stress signals are relayed by the hypothalamus and pituitary in the brain to the adrenal glands (in the kidneys) triggering the release of a stress hormone named cortisol. Throughout this process (known as the sympathetic nervous system or fight-or-flight response) heart and breath rate accelerate, muscles tense, and pupils dilate.

In the short term, cortisol turns off the immune system; however, when stress is prolonged for lengthy periods of time, the immune system becomes desensitized to the release of cortisol resulting in heightened and sustained immune system activity. Through this process, depression and chronic psychological distress induces a sustained low-grade inflammation, which in turn accelerates one's risk for a variety of difficult physical health concerns of diseases.

Higher PIL has been shown to facilitate changes in the inflammatory response, specifically by influencing interleukin-6 (IL-6), a proinflammatory cytokine that is vital for immune system response to a variety of bacteria and illnesses. The dysregulation of IL-6 has emerged as a mechanism involved in numerous neurological conditions, including multiple sclerosis and Alzheimer's diseases. One experiment examining blood levels of IL-6 and its receptor (CD 126) in adult women found that higher PIL scores were associated with lower levels of CD 126, signifying less IL-6 activity.[90]

In a 2021 longitudinal investigation, Anne-Josee Guimond and colleagues identified another biological link between purpose and

Measuring Purpose

inflammatory response in the form of C-reactive protein, an annular protein detected in blood levels that shows heightened concentration in response to bodily inflammation. The researchers found that higher PIL at baseline was associated with lower levels of C-reactive protein at 8-years follow-up.[91]

The strong link identified between purpose in life and vital health outcomes should inspire further research into PIL in the near future. Given that heightened purpose serves as a buffer against cognitive decline, improves psychological well-being, and reduces inflammatory markers within the blood, there are several exciting opportunities for future research in this field:

1) The use of lengthier and developmental studies to determine how changes in PIL over time (related to life circumstances) influence vital measurements of health. This will allow a better determination of the specific stage in a person's life that it may be most important to establish high levels of purpose.

2) The influence of strategies or interventions for heightening sense of purpose and subsequent effects on health outcomes in individuals of all ages. Identifying the strategies or therapies that stimulate a strong perception of purpose could hold a very important key in treating chronic illnesses

It is without question that pharmaceutical treatments for physical and mental health issues have helped countless individuals to heal from these illnesses and live with enhanced quality and longevity. However, they have limited effectiveness for some individuals and can also engender significant side effects. Hopefully the medical community will make a conscious effort to examine PIL and recommend practices and lifestyle habits that will promote higher levels of purpose. A broader emphasis on practices that promote holistic well-being would lead to significantly lower indices of disease, resulting in a lessened burden on our healthcare system.

Purpose can be a tremendous tool for finding physical and mental resilience during the most challenging of circumstances. Research is emerging to show that purpose and its pursuit are moderated by specific activation patterns and neural networks in the human brain. This line of research lends support to the hypothesis that humans are hardwired to strive for purpose. Additionally, the physical and mental ramifications of perceived purpose levels demonstrate that finding purpose may be one of the most important missions of the human experience.

Neurological Correlates of Purpose

Regarding research on the neurological mechanisms involved in purpose, it is important to note that the majority of studies have focused on the concepts of happiness and overall well-being rather than purpose directly. The construct of happiness can be categorized into two components; hedonia (temporary pleasure or reward in the absence of distress) as well as eudemonia (pleasure from a goal achieved or a life well-lived). Eudomania is a greek word and principal component of the philosophical teachings of Plato and Socrates. These philosophers believed that eudomania reflects the highest aim of moral thought and conduct. Unfortunately, this term is often translated from Greek to simply mean "happiness", but that is inaccurate and misleading. The word happy is derived from the Norse word "happ", which more closely relates to chance, fortune, and luck. Another word for happy in Old English is "gesaelig", which over centuries has turned into the modern word "silly".

However, eudomania has nothing to do with silliness or luck, or even short-term joy or pleasure. It has everything to do with thought and attention that leads into a life that is worthwhile, fulfilling, and purposeful. Many philosophical schools including the Hellenistic consider eudaimonia the highest good, and the very aim and purpose of philosophy. In contrast to happiness, eudaimonia is not an emotion but rather a state of doing (per Aristotle).

It eventually leads to satisfaction and fulfillment of the highest kind, but it does not originate with or depend on pleasure. University of Ottawa scholar Veronika Huta analyzed a multitude of definitions and translations relating to eudainomia and hedonia in the 2016 Novel *Pursuing Eudaimonia Versus Hedonia: Distinctions, Similarities, and Relationships.* In summary, eudaimonia encompasses aspects of life like authenticity (acting in accord with one's deepest values), meaning (understanding a bigger picture), excellence (striving for higher quality in one's behavior, performance, and achievement), and personal growth (self-actualization and maturation).

Hedonia in contrast, is related to pleasure, enjoyment, and satisfaction in the here and now, and in the absence of distress.[92] Currently, most of the research on neural mechanisms involved in happiness have focused on capturing hedonia or reward, especially as it pertains to typical aspects of the human experience like addiction, attraction, and hunger. Notably, there is some degree of overlap between hedonia and edaimonia, and that is also true to some extent for the neural mechanisms that mediate them.

Measuring Purpose

However, there are some notable neurological differences between these constructs that will be discussed. Kent Berridge and colleagues have shown that neural activations in the ventral striatal circuitry (within the nucleus accumbens and ventral pallidum) are activated in paradigms that evoke wanting, liking, and prediction components of the same reward. The ventral striatum is a critical deep subcortical region that is heavily involved in reward-salience and addiction.

The typical paradigm for studying neural activation with hedonia consists of participants being presented with a text phrase that has been rated as highly positive or exciting (e.g., winning the lottery). They are subsequently asked to visualize images relating to this text for 12 seconds during which brain activation is assessed using fMRI (a technique that determines which areas of the brain activate during a task by assessing blood flow to certain anatomical areas).

In one investigation, when positive imagery was compared with unpleasant imagery (e.g. losing one's job) the connectivity between the nucleus accumbens and amygdala, and between the ventral prefrontal cortex and amygdala was significantly increased during the positive compared to negative imagery conditions.[93] The ventral prefrontal cortex is critical for the representation of reinforcement expectancies and both positive and negative emotional regulation.

Additionally, activation during positive emotional stimuli was increased in the nucleus accumbens and ventromedial frontal cortex (implicated in self-control and morality) relative to negative-emotional stimuli. In another paradigm, Davidson and colleagues recorded new mothers soon after the birth of their first child in an fMRI scanner while they processed images of either their own infants, a stranger infant, or a stranger adult. The greatest ventral prefrontal activation occurred in response to pictures of their own infants. These mothers also reported the highest positive mood ratings in response to these images.[94] These studies focused on neural activation elicited by short-duration emotional stimuli; however, it remains unclear if these short-term neural responses correlate with more persisting forms of happiness such as meaning and purpose or whether other forms of neural activation or connectivity are better predictors of these constructs. Additionally, the studies all focused on happiness or positive affect, yet more enduring forms of well-being (e.g., purpose) often involve trials and tribulations or successfully overcoming various elements of adversity.

Richard Davidson and colleagues have posited that the best evidence for distinct neurological bases of these two forms of happiness can be found in studies investigating neural mechanisms that manifest depression, especially considering the inverse relation between depressive levels and purpose. Anhedonia, or a loss of pleasure or interest in relation to previously enjoyable hobbies or activities is a key component of depression. While some theorists believe that anhedonia involves a reduced capacity for pleasure, an alternative explanation posits that anhedonia is mediated by an inability to sustain positive affect across longer time intervals.

To test this hypothesis, a 2009 study investigated activation patterns in response to positive emotional images in depressed participants compared to non-depressed controls. Both depressed participants and controls showed similar activation in the reward-related brain regions (e.g., ventral striatum/nucleus accumbens) to single positive emotional images. However, when the researchers examined sustained activation in the nucleus accumbens across repeated trials of positive-eliciting images, significant differences emerged between the two groups. As the trials continued in the task, control participants were able to maintain sustained activation in the nucleus accumbens, however the depressed patients showed a gradual extinction of response in this region.[95]

Further, the decreased capacity for response was related to lower levels of self-reported positive affect while viewing the images. Lastly, when connectivity between different brain areas was examined a frontal-striatal network which showed sustained activation among the controls tailed off with progressive trials in the depressed patients. This network has been established as a vital mediator of cognitive and psychological processes tied to well-being.

Intriguingly, the authors conducted a follow-up study and found that when antidepressant medications were administered the ability to sustain ventral tegmental area activation directly correlated with reports of positive affect shift among clinically depressed patients. The ventral tegmental area (VTA) is closely connected with the nucleus accumbens and plays a significant role in reward, cognition, and motivation.

Using a large community sample, Davidson and colleagues examined the associations between psychological well-being and individual differences in sustained activation in the ventral striatum. Individuals displaying the marker of higher levels of sustained attention in the ventral striatum across trials containing positive images reported higher levels of psychological well-being. Notably, these authors also found that sustained activation in the dorsolateral prefrontal cortex during stimuli processing was related to higher levels of well-being and positive emotionality.

The dorsolateral prefrontal cortex is a region of the brain critically involved with executive functioning abilities as well as emotional regulation. The researchers also examined the relationship between activity in these brain regions and an individual's cortisol levels over a 24-hour timeframe. Cortisol is the body's key stress hormone that is triggered by the sympathetic nervous response, and higher levels indicate greater physiological stress experienced. The researchers found that lower levels of detected cortisol were predicted by greater sustained activation in both the ventral striatum and the dorsolateral prefrontal region. These findings suggest that a sustained and prolonged high activation in the DLPFC and ventral striatum is critical for more enduring forms of psychological well-being with cortisol regulation as a potential mediator.[94]

Using an innovative paradigm, Eva Telzer and colleagues of the University of North Carolina studied brain activation (via fMRI) in response to two tasks; one that engaged hedonic happiness and another that captured eudaimonic happiness. In the eudaimonic task, participants could earn money for themselves and their families by responding to a series of financial offers that varied in terms of whether they represented gains or losses for the participants or their families. In essence, the task captured neural activation during the process of making a donation to the family that involved self-sacrifice, thus capturing a meaningful prosocial behavior.

The hedonic task was the Balloon Analog Risk Task in which a participant was shown a computerized balloon and given the choice to inflate the balloon on each trial, which can either make it grow larger or explode. The more the balloon is inflated, the greater the monetary reward becomes, but in turn there is a higher the risk for explosion. The authors found that ventral striatal activation in response to the task that engaged eudaimonic happiness predicted lower depressive symptoms over the course of two years, while activation in the ventral striatum during the hedonic reward (balloon) task was not an important predictor of depressive symptoms during this time span.

This study provides support for the importance of ventral striatal activation as well as the context of the task presented when considering neural networks involved with happiness and purpose. Given what is already known about depression, well-being, and purpose it is likely the case that neural markers of eudaimonic happiness are also closely tied to purpose in life, while markers involved with hedonistic happiness are not as relevant.[96]

Another hallmark aspect of the psychological construct of purpose is experiencing and overcoming some degree of adversity and personal struggle. Dr. Viktor Frankl explained that despair is the equivalent to suffering without purpose. If a person cannot find meaning in their suffering, they will tend to despair. However, if a person can find a way to uncover meaning in their adversity, they can turn tribulations into an achievement, finding great psychological value along the way. Psychological resilience is essential for achieving this kind of deeper purpose. Resilience is the process of successfully adapting to difficult life experiences through mental, emotional, and behavioral regulation. In the wise words of Chinese philosopher Confucius "Our greatest glory is not in never falling, but in rising every time we fall."

Measuring Purpose

The majority of the work on the neural networks involved in resilience is being conducted with rodents, which is understandable and preferable given the need to experimentally manipulate difficult or overwhelming situations that can be overcome by an organism. The study procedures usually involve measures of recovery following negative events with the time needed to recover serving as the typical indicator of one's physical or psychological well-being. Given the amygdala's strong involvement in fear and anxious response, activation in this area is often used to conceptualize rate of recovery (and resilience) from an adverse event. Faster recovery within this brain region (reduced activation) has been linked with adaptive coping to adversity and diminished fear, stress, and anxiety to a challenging stimulus.

In studies on mice exposed to predators or chronic defeat stressors, those exhibiting more behavioral resilience also showed higher levels of early gene expression in glutamatergic neurons in the medial prefrontal cortex (commonly implicated in social and emotional regulation).[97] Consistent with this finding, research in macaque monkeys has shown that directly stimulating the medial prefrontal cortex promotes resilience to social defeat stress.[98] Together, these results highlight the important role of the amygdala and medial PFC in psychological resilience. It is likely the case that the medial PFC can effectively inhibit amygdala response when it is functioning optimally.

In one human investigation, a large sample of middle-aged adults completed an automatic emotion regulation paradigm in which positive, negative, or neutral pictures were presented for four seconds, after which a neutral face was presented either one or three seconds following the image, or not at all. Brain activation patterns were recorded using fMRI. Three days after the session, participants rated the likeability of the faces they had seen, along with novel unfamiliar faces that served as control images. In assessing response to the emotional pictures, the researchers measured amygdala activity during the four-second processing stage (reactivity) as well as the four seconds after the image disappeared (recovery).

The researchers found that increases in the big five personality trait "neuroticism" (which positively relates to negative affect and negatively relates to well-being) were predicted by stronger amygdala activation during the recovery period, but not during the reactivity period.[99]

These findings suggest that a person's initial physiological response to a negative event has little to do with neuroticism, well-being, and resilience; however, the recovery of the nervous system (amygdala) is an important modulator of these processes and is a key predictor of resilience and ultimate well-being. In summary, being able to soothe the fear response (amygdala) is vitally important for long-term recovery and mitigating chronic inflammation. Ultimately, this can lead to greater purpose and happiness.

Chapter 7:

A Personal Journey to Purpose

A Tale of Perceived Purposelessness and Intoxicating Fear

When I was still a collegiate tennis player in the Spring of 2015, I was engaged in a strenuous tennis practice with one of my teammates that remains a good friend to this day. It was a quiet Saturday morning on campus, and we were logging some extra repetitions outside of the NCAA's allotted practice hours. We had high hopes to close out our senior season and last hoorah with a conference championship trophy in our hands. Approximately an hour and a half into our practice, I suddenly felt an unfamiliar feeling of suffocation. I had been out of breath on a tennis court on more occasions than I care to admit, but as I tried to inhale slowly with the hopes of catching my breath, I felt an intense tightness and pressure in my chest, almost as though a WWE wrestler was pushing against it with all their might.

As I frantically continued this unsuccessful process, I simply could not catch my breath to the point of satisfaction. Suddenly, my vision became fuzzy, my heart began beating like a bongo drum, and I felt the intense feeling that the world was spinning upside down or that I was fading away from reality.

I was no stranger to the sensation of a panic attack, as I had experienced a surge of anxiety nearly 8 years earlier as a 14-year-old child, shortly after my parents had informed me that we would be moving from the suburbs of Chicago to South Florida prior to my freshman year of high school. The intense reaction I had to that announcement coupled with the loss of a fellow classmate to cancer had my emotions swirling intensely, with a strong bias towards the negative. It was around that time that I began experiencing panic attacks in the school setting so constantly that I missed five consecutive school days at one point and began to lose hope that I would be able to graduate 8th grade with my classmates and friends. Over the course of several months, I overcame the intense panic attacks I was experiencing with help from my family and friends, as well as some useful cognitive and meditative techniques I learned in therapy sessions.

The helplessness I felt as a 14-year-old child possessing a very limited knowledge on the concept of mental illness is what made me want to one day enter the field of psychology. When I first experienced a panic attack, I thought I was either dying or completely losing control of my mind and body. My lack of awareness and poor coping skills made me wonder how many millions of other children, adolescents, and adults experience the profound effects of mental health issues without proper knowledge or understanding of what they are experiencing, as well as any sort of access to quality clinical care. I was fortunate to have met a helpful, professional therapist at this stage of my life and I am forever grateful for their assistance. I also have tremendous love and gratitude for the assistance and patience of my mother who has experienced her own bouts with mental health issues and was always available to listen and provide sound advice.

This life experience as a 14-year-old ignited a passion in me to study psychology, become a mental health advocate and provider, and one-day help others to feel equipped and powerful in overcoming the suffocating grip of mental health issues. Fast forward 8 years into the future, and just a few months away from graduating with a BA in psychology, and I was once again grasping for breath and clutching at my chest. However, this time the physical symptoms were not a manifestation of anxiety or stressful life experience (or so I thought at least).

After 10 or 15 minutes, my friend accompanied me to the main athletic building to see one of the trainers who subsequently gave me some electrolyte pills and said my breathing issues were likely due to a muscle cramp in my chest. I was not entirely convinced and remained vigilant in trying to determine why I had experienced this sharp and unusual discomfort. The next day I went to practice at the usual time and about 30 minutes into the practice while we were drilling cross court forehands, I felt the same tightness in my chest and trouble getting a full breath in.

I tried my best to work through the discomfort and finish practice until I felt some familiar waves of panic pulsing through me. I went to see the trainer again afterwards, and once again was assured that it was likely due to cramps brought on by the unusual heat wave hitting Charlotte at the time. At this point, my mind was extremely fixated on the discomfort and my inability to experience a full breath of air. My mind began to travel to some really dark places including the fear that I had a terminal illness.

For the next week of practice, a vicious cycle continued with me experiencing pain and discomfort, the trainers finding nothing wrong, and me feeling strong waves of anxiety throughout the rest of the day. Finally, I was able to get an appointment to see the lead sports doctor at the University. During examination, he felt around my chest and located a mass about the size of a golf ball. It was located just below my collar bone which protrudes out naturally, so it was not as easy to detect as it sounds. Once he found the spot and started examining it, I could tell that this was the likely source of the pain. He said he couldn't say for sure what it was and ordered a chest x-ray for me. Needless to say, I was very concerned at this point and naturally my mind was going to some catastrophic possibilities.

I was filled with so much drive and motivation to finish my senior season on a high note and graduate in just a few months; however, I could not suppress the continuous flow of intrusive and negative thoughts relating to the injury. I was becoming increasingly distant from my girlfriend and teammates, and I could hardly focus for three minutes at a time on my studies and part-time job as a tutor. The questions flooding my headspace included, would this be a setback that could prevent me from finishing school and graduating? Could this be an issue that would take my life away? Was I spiraling out of control and losing my mind completely?

Reflecting back, I was also experiencing an onslaught of stress from other life circumstances at the time. I was eagerly waiting to see if I would be accepted into any graduate programs in psychology, a necessary step for obtaining the sort of jobs I was striving for. Therefore, there was much uncertainty about where I would be living next year, what I would be studying, and whether my girlfriend at the time and I would be able to stay together given the uncertainty of the circumstances. My parents were also going through some difficulties in their relationship and so I felt some pressure to move back to South Florida to be more accessible to my little sisters and entire family.

I had very much become a creature of habit and a routine-oriented individual over the last few years with a pretty rigorous tennis, scholastic, and work schedule. Looking back on this time, I do think I would have handled the chest injury better had my stress levels not already been so elevated. I also must admit that I was not practicing what I was preaching as a psychology student and advocate. I was setting aside almost no time to engage in positive activities for promoting mental health such as meditation, journaling, and deep breathing.

By the time I got to Charlotte Medical Center for the X-ray I was unraveling quickly. My mind constantly defaulted to fear and anxiety, and I was no longer the positive and easy-going person that my peers had known me to be. Frequent panic attacks (15-20-per-day) were triggered by the shortness of breath I was feeling and the uncertainty of the situation. Finally, the X-ray came back, and I was diagnosed with a very rare injury in the chest called costochondritis (kos-toe-kon-DRY-tis). Costochondritis is technically an inflammation of the cartilage that connects the rib to the breastbone (sternum). Pain caused by costochondritis is thought to mimic that of a heart attack, lung disease, or osteoarthritis. Fortunately, the pain and swelling associated with the condition does not actually restrict or hinder the ability to breathe; however, it does typically lead the person experiencing it to feel completely out of breath or unable to take a full breath.

Although I was relieved that the X-ray was negative, the news of having a rare condition involving swollen cartilage in the chest cavity that is basically incurable did not tremendously ease the anxiety I was feeling. The presence of this condition also meant that I would be experiencing sharp pain every time I practiced the sport that I loved. Despite experiencing some frustrating losses over the years, tennis had represented "my happy place" since I was 5 years old.

The presence of this injury and the uncertainty surrounding it would serve as a catalyst to a debilitating episode of mental health anguish. Following the injury, I was overtaken by fear that I had a terminal illness and mistakenly took towards researching my symptoms using google, as though I had learned nothing from my psychology training the prior 4 years… Automatically, anything related to shortness of breath and chest pain was met with a wide array of terminal illness possibilities. This sudden fear about health and uncertainty about the future made me intensely aware of my own mortality again. It caused me to think about the possibility of my own death with constant frequency.

It is extremely normal to have these thoughts from time to time, but they were invading my mind constantly to the point that I had thoughts like, "If I could fall ill and pass away suddenly, then what is the point of everything I am doing" or "If me and everyone I know will eventually pass away, then what is the point of anything we do on earth".

These very bleak and nihilistic thoughts took a stronghold of my headspace and made my waking hours very difficult to endure. I was experiencing something that both myself and my loved ones had difficulty understanding. I was fearful that maybe no one else would understand. However, I was very wrong.

The Fear of the Unknown and the Uncontrollable

Thanatophobia is the term used to describe excessive fear of death or the process of dying. A person with thanatophobia may experience high anxiety and distress when thinking about their own death or the concept in general as well as feelings of anger, guilt, or agitation. Although research and awareness on this topic are not well-developed, one disorder in which death anxiety may be a central component is obsessive-compulsive disorder (OCD). In fact, the fear of death has been found to emerge across various subtypes of the disorder.[100] Although there is no established consensus on the number of distinct subtypes of OCD, certain presentations have been commonly identified including contaminate, compulsive checking, and pure obsessions. The contaminate subtype commonly relates to compulsive washing or cleaning behaviors. Self-report studies of individuals with contamination concerns reveal that death fears are a driving force behind their compulsions, as washing occurs in response to fear that exposure to germs and contamination may result in fatal illness.

Compulsive checking is the other most prevalent subtype of OCD and approximately 75% of those with this subtype report that checking concerns in the environment serves the purpose of preventing "something bad" from occurring in the future. In line with this explanation, those who compulsively check stovetops, locks on front doors or garages, as well as lights or power outlets, are engaging in behaviors that are motivated by fears of household fires, electrocution, or intruder invasions. Compulsions may also revolve around checking that family members are safe, or repeatedly checking that they have not inadvertently killed someone, such as by retracing a traffic route they have driven.

Some individuals with OCD experience intrusive and concerning obsessions, without typical compulsive or ritualistic behaviors. Common themes in this form of OCD (often referred to as "Pure O") include sex, religion, and violence. Although there may be a less obvious connection in this form of OCD, death anxiety may still be an important driving force. For example, some individuals cope with intrusive thoughts revolving around various forms of physical harm to self or others.

Death anxiety has also been theorized to play a key role in the construct of indecisiveness which is heavily involved in OCD. Indecisiveness is closely related to perfectionism and high levels of conscientiousness. Although perfectionism can be problematic at high levels it may cultivate a sense of achievement or control, in all facets of life including risk of death. Therefore, death anxiety may be a driving force in presentations of OCD involving high levels of indecisiveness and where decisions are constantly questioned or re-rehearsed. Notably, chronic fear of death has likely been a strong mediator of the increased prevalence of OCD (2% to 4%) occurring since the onset of COVID-19.

A Personal Journey

As I began to spiral downward, the fear I was experiencing became closely intertwined with my negative feelings about college ending, and the likelihood of living many miles and in some cases continents away from some of my teammates and close friends. This spawned an obsession with time passing, and more specifically a fear of time passing too quickly. The fear of time itself or time passing is referred to as chronophobia.

With regards to phobia (an overwhelming and debilitating fear of just about anything that evokes this response in an individual) there are three main categories including agoraphobia, social phobia, and specific phobias which commonly includes spiders, snakes, public speaking, and heights. Chronophobia would most appropriately fall under the category of a specific phobia because time is a specific object or concept that one can be fearful of. Chronophobia is especially common in prison inmates, elderly populations, and individuals battling a terminal illness, but it can manifest in any person who has an extreme amount of stress and anxiety in their life.

According to Peter Annas and Paul Lichtenstein, chronophobia can be caused by a traumatic experience in one's childhood, genetics, incarceration, or old age. Such traumatic experiences can lead to a withdrawal from one's reality through means of dissociation, depersonalization, or derealization.[101] This can lead to heightened conscious awareness of time passing slower or faster than what is to be expected. Incarcerated prisoners are more likely to experience chronophobia (sometimes referred to as prison neurosis) because they are acutely aware of the timeframe of their sentence and often become obsessed with counting down the days until their freedom.

A Personal Journey

They may also possess a deep fear that they have wasted their life (or time on earth) and that they will not have a chance for redemption. Common symptoms they may have include delusions, dissatisfaction with life, claustrophobia, depression, and feelings of panic and madness. Elderly individuals are also more likely to cope with chronophobia because they may perceive that they are running out of time or due to an intense desire to fulfill goals and dreams before their time runs out. When they feel that their lives are near the end, they start to fear time because it threatens their existence. This fear is similar to chronoperception because it includes the idea that the speed of brain function depends on the metabolic rate in the hypothalamus. As people get older, their metabolism slows. The elderly may believe that as a result of their slowing metabolism, their brains do not function as well, which makes them more chronophobic. Chronophobia will similarly affect a greater proportion of individuals with terminal illnesses or those who possess a pervasive fear that they may have one.

Chronophobia was also depicted in Washington Irving's 1993 novel *Rip Van Winkle* which tells a fictional story of a man that had fallen asleep for 20 years and wakes to an entirely new world and personal reality. Most of the people he knew and loved, including his wife and friends are now gone and this overwhelming change of life circumstances sends him into waves of fear and panic revolving around this passing of time.

With time, his chronophobia is eventually cured when he realizes that despite the tremendous changes in his environment his core beliefs and purpose are still intact. He is able to make new friends and become re-acclimated into society by the end of the novel. At this point in time, chronophobia is not a condition that is well-understood or studied empirically.

It is considered to be a specific phobia; however, it seems reasonable to conclude that this is a more abstract fear than something like a phobia to a specific creature (snake) or situation (heights). Time is so intricately intertwined in our day-to-day life and time passing is one of the aspects of the human experience that no matter how hard we push and try, we cannot gain control over. Although this has not been supported through research, I would hypothesize that chronophobia and thanatophobia are a manifestation of the same underlying condition. Ultimately, mortality and time passing are two unchangeable aspects of the human experience that can leave all of us looking for answers, feeling despair, and trying to relinquish some element of control in our lives; this may be especially difficult for individuals with OCD-like symptoms or a clinical diagnosis of this condition.

I would also argue that chronophobia and thanatophobia are both deeply influenced by issues or skirmishes with the psychological construct of purpose. I have drawn from both personal and professional experiences to reach this conclusion. When I was 22 years old and fearing for my life due to a rare injury with frightening physical symptoms, I was coping with so much uncertainty about my future. At the same time, my valued purposes of being a college tennis player and diligent college student were both reaching a conclusion.

Lastly, I was in limbo about my future academic and professional opportunities as well as my relationship status with a very supportive and wonderful partner. I have recently come to terms with the fact that the combination of all these circumstances was perceived by my 22-year-old self as an overwhelming threat to my purpose in life. Suddenly, my psychological well-being had taken a severe negative turn because of the stress I was feeling in response to this attack. Working at a neuropsychology center for the last two years with over 600 clients coping with depression, anxiety, OCD, and substance abuse has taught me that a core commonality exists among many of these individuals. This includes the perception that purpose is lacking or that purpose is under attack from uncontrollable forces in their lives.

Notably, I would like to point out that the stressors I faced as a 22-year-old pale in comparison to some of the true terrors my clients have experienced or that people living in war zones, impoverished neighborhoods, or abusive familial relationships must endure. Still, stress is in the eye of the beholder and whether a situation is deemed as high-stress or low-stress to outside perspectives is of little relevance to the individual whose mind and body may be perceiving a tremendous threat. Many other practitioners and researchers since Viktor Frankl have also held the perspective that a perceived purposelessness in life can lead to internalizing and externalizing elements of mental illness including Richard Davidson, Eric Kim, Jonathan Haidt, Jordan Peterson, and David Kessler.[102]

Based on this framework, a natural conclusion could be drawn that people who are relatively "unsuccessful" in their career, social life, or romantic relationships would perceive a lack of purpose, and thus develop a mental health concern. However, countless individuals who are very successful in their careers including doctors, lawyers, athletes, and even politicians struggle with various mental health injuries. Additionally, individuals who are married and have large sources of social support can still experience depression, anxiety, or ADHD. Mental health issues do not discriminate and there is a strong role of both genetics and environmental influences in the development of these conditions. One possibility is that individuals who are susceptible to mental health concerns tend to think about and ask questions related to deep philosophical issues such as "why and how did I get here, or what is my purpose in existing"?

Both anxiety and depressive levels have been associated with higher levels of trait neuroticism in adults and adolescents.[103] Neuroticism is a fundamental personality trait that comprises one-fifth of the Big 5 personality inventory along with extraversion, agreeableness, conscientiousness, and openness. Individuals scoring high in neuroticism are more likely to perceive situations as stressful, dangerous, and frustrating, and are also more likely to feel loneliness.

Individuals high in neuroticism are also more careful in their decision making and less likely to engage in high-risk activities, potentially serving an evolutionary benefit in socio-historical eras of turbulence. Still, higher levels of neuroticism may be the key link to increased fear of the unknown which often occurs in individuals coping with anxiety and depression. A 2022 investigation in India found that higher levels of neuroticism predicted increased death anxiety as well as anxiety related to the COVID-19 pandemic.[104]

It would be advantageous to conduct a developmental study where children between the ages of 5 and 8 years are surveyed on how often they think about deep philosophical issues. These same children could be tracked during their adolescent and early adulthood years to explore the prevalence of mental health concerns and how this is related to their proclivity for pondering topics of mortality, faith, meaning, and purpose as children. Personality traits could also be examined as possible mediators of this relationship.

Individuals that are prone to mood disorders may fixate more on the unknown and the uncontrollable throughout their lives. Thus, it is incredibly important for these individuals to learn strategies for calming their mind and mitigating their fears. It is also imperative that these individuals develop the perception that their existence matters and is purposeful.

In the years since the existential crisis of my early 20's I have effectively integrated these practices into my life. I am incredibly grateful for the support and wisdom provided to me by therapists, coaches, professors, friends, and family. In the present day, I make a conscious effort to get sufficient sleep (7-8 hours a night), exercise frequently (5-6 times per week), and practice daily meditation and breathing exercises (Wim Hoff breathing or box breathing). I also engage in frequent prayer and strive for a healthier work/life balance, ensuring that I get to do the leisure activities I love such as playing tennis, fishing, and surfing. When I started to prioritize my own mental health, I became significantly happier, and my life is more purposeful. I am also happily married to the love of my life, and yes, it is the girl I have referenced throughout this book. I still cope with fear and anxiety pertaining to the unknown, but I focus my energy and attention on the things I can control and above all living in the present moment. I feel that I am no longer lost and that I have great purpose in my life. Many

A Personal Journey

of the strategies presented in the next chapter have been beneficial for my journey and I hope you find them beneficial as well.

Chapter 8:

Treatment Options for Restoring Purpose

When I was in my first year of graduate school, I was particularly drawn to TED talks on psychology. This was partially because the messages were extremely informative, and also because my mind needed something that could be digested in 10 or 15 minutes due to attentional fatigue from reading 5-10 scientific journal articles a day. There was a talk titled "The Most Important Lessons Learned From 83,000 Brain Scans" by Dr. Daniel Amen that especially grabbed my attention and made a lasting impact on my views within the field of psychiatry. I had known countless individuals (including friends, family, and teammates) that had dealt with mental health issues and not even one of them had been prescribed a brain scan to assess a possible neurological origin of their ailments. Brain scans represent an excellent strategy to systematically make the field of psychiatry more medical. In the words of Daniel Amen, this approach will make the process of selecting medications or other treatment modalities "less like throwing darts at a dartboard in the dark".[105]

This introductory TED talk details the value of single-photon emission computerized tomography (SPECT) scans for aiding in the recognition of cognitive decline, depression, anxiety, OCD, ADHD, and more. Traditionally, a tremendous portion of psychiatric diagnoses have been made using only self-reported symptoms from patients. Unfortunately, patients may not be the most accurate reporters, especially considering the impact that their mental health issue is likely having on their mental clarity.

I firmly believe in the importance of accurate diagnoses, especially when intervention approaches are used such as psychotropic medications or direct brain stimulation that are accompanied with problematic side effects when administered incorrectly. Therefore, the use of a brain imaging technique is of tremendous value in conjunction to the administration of detailed cognitive and psychiatric evaluations.

For anyone that is seeking mental health care for the onset of symptoms that are relatively new (this is common with the unprecedented events the past few years), I would highly recommend trying to obtain a detailed assessment along with a brain scan for diagnosis. There are many innovative treatment options in existence but the best way to customize these treatments is by first gaining a better understanding of one's unique psychological and neurophysiological traits.

When working with clients I frequently use Quantitative Electroencephalography (qEEG), which is a clinical brain activity scan that helps to evaluate overall brain health and identify characteristics that link to common psychiatric conditions and symptoms. This technology enables an examination of an individual's brain activity patterns compared to a typical activation profile for one's given age and gender, in 20 key areas of the brain. Although it does not allow as precise of a spatial examination as SPECT or MRI, there are numerous benefits to using qEEG in clinical contexts.

1) It is completely non-invasive and emits no radiation whatsoever. As a result, it can be used with children and with unlimited use when tracking a patient's progress as a function of an intervention tool. 2) The scans are typically priced anywhere from 150-300$ making them much more affordable than MRI and SPECT scans. Hopefully, in the near future major insurance companies will also assist with out-of-pocket payments for these treatments. 3) There is an entire database of qEEG scans published by Dr. Robert Thatcher which allows a comparison of one's activation patterns to what is considered "typical" for someone of their respective age and gender.

The qEEG allows an examination of delta (0 to 4 Hz), theta (4 to 7 Hz), alpha (8 to 12 Hz), and beta (13 to 30 Hz) activity waves. Delta is prominently observed when a person is in a deep sleep while theta is the dominant activation pattern when a person is in a drowsy or meditative state. Alpha is considered to be the default state of brain activity (calm and engaged in self-directed thought) and represents the middle ground of the EEG activation spectrum.

When excessive amounts of delta, theta, and sometimes alpha (mid-range) activities are detected in the left frontal, temporal, or parietal regions, this is a strong marker for symptoms of depression including low mood, anhedonia, and difficulties with concentration. Further, increased slow wave activation (delta and theta) bilaterally in the frontal cortex is commonly a marker for ADHD in young children as well as cognitive decline in older adults. When beta (the fast-wave frequency involved in high alertness) is depleted in the frontal cortex this could also be indicative of ADHD and cognitive issues. When excessive beta is detected throughout the cortex and especially in the right frontal, temporal, or parietal areas this is a marker of over arousal and may signify the presence of generalized anxiety, panic, OCD, or insomnia. Notably, there is an asymmetry in the brain in which the left hemisphere mediates positive emotionality and approach behaviors while the right hemisphere is more involved in withdrawal behaviors and negative emotionality.[106]

The end result of the 30-minute brain activity scan is a sequence of detailed color images of the brain showing the degree of abnormality present in any of the aforementioned activity types based on standard deviations from average levels. Preliminary evidence has shown that qEEG findings can predict response to different classes of medications. For example, individuals showing excessive theta activity bilaterally in the frontal cortex had better response to stimulants (Adderall, Ritalin); however, those with increased left frontal alpha activation showed better response to SSRI's (Prozac, Zoloft, Lexapro).[107]Additionally, brain-based therapeutics (such as TMS and neurofeedback) are better customized for each patient using qEEG.

Psychiatric Medications

Since lithium was first introduced in the 1950's (roughly 70 years ago), the dominant approach for altering biological mechanisms relating to mental health issues has been using psychotropic medications. Today, the most prescribed psychotropic medications are antidepressants; particularly Zoloft or sertraline (41.4 million), Celexa or citalopram (39.4 million); Prozac or fluozetine (28.3 million) and Lexapro or escitalopram (24.9) million. There has been feverous debate regarding the efficacy and appropriateness of antidepressant medications in the last 15 years after a 2008 meta-analysis on 35 prior studies published by Dr. Irving Kirsh concluded that there was "little evidence to support the prescription of antidepressant medication to any but the most severely depressed patients".

He went on to report that for individuals with moderate depression, the results were comparable to placebo effects and only those with very severe cases could reap benefits.[108] Additionally, popular writer Johann Hari published a rather scathing criticism of antidepressants, and the field of psychiatry in general in his 2018 best-selling novel *Lost Connections: Uncovering the Real Causes of Depression - and the Unexpected Solutions.* This novel received praise from notable individuals like Elton John, Hillary Clinton, and Russell Brand.[109]

A comprehensive 2018 meta-analysis was published in Lancet by Dr. Andrea Cipriani and colleagues to add additional scientific merit to this debate. The study was the most comprehensive review to date, examining 522 randomized clinical trials and assessing the efficacy of 21 different antidepressants delivered to over 100,000 patients. The article concluded that antidepressants significantly reduce symptoms (50% or more) in approximately 60% of individuals with moderate to severe depression when taken properly for the minimum amount of time (2 months).[110] These results suggest that antidepressants are an effective tool for helping patients cope with mental health concerns when taken properly and have likely helped countless individuals to improve their quality of life. Notably, Dr. Cipriani had no conflict of interests as the study was funded by the National Institute for Health Research with no funding provided by the pharmaceutical industry. Additionally, one of the co-authors, Dr. John Ioannidis from Stanford had vocally opposed the use of antidepressants in the past, further showing the unbiased agenda of the research team.

Still the long-term effects of these treatments remain poorly understood. The Sequenced Treatment Alternatives to Relieve Depression (STAR*D) investigation on 3,671 patients included a one-year-follow up and found that although approximately 65% of participants achieved remission through antidepressants, roughly 40% of these participants experienced relapse in the following 10 months.[111] This means that roughly 26% percent of the participants maintained response to the medication over the course of the following year. Additionally, one study estimated that 40% of patients taking antidepressants develop concerning side effects including worsening depression, anxiety, tremors, dizziness, headaches, migraines, and loss of libido. Two of the most common (sexual side effects and weight gain) are often concerning enough to cause people to stop taking these drugs.

The Power of Magnetic Energy

Due to the mixed results on the long-term use and potential for side effects with antidepressant medications, it is highly advantageous and necessary to explore alternative treatment options for psychiatric patients. This is especially important for patients with chronic conditions that are treatment-resistant to both medications and various forms of talk therapy. Given the recent discoveries relating to the neuroanatomy of depression (in addition to well-being and purpose); a promising treatment approach involves directly targeting these focal areas though a brain stimulating technology known as transcranial magnetic stimulation (TMS).

In the last 15 years, TMS has been pulsing with popularity due to its ability to stimulate different areas of the brain in a non-invasive manner. The treatment for depression which consists of 36 daily sessions was the first to receive FDA approval back in 2008 and has now received approval with 12 different TMS devices. The traditional TMS approach utilizes a figure-8 coil to deliver the electromagnetic pulses to different areas of the brain.

A highly innovative company named Brainsway patented a new coil configuration (H-coil) that is able to reach 3.2 cm deep in the brain compared to the traditional .7 cm deep with figure-8 coil.[113] This has enabled the targeting of deeper brain areas such as the anterior cingulate cortex and striatum (obsessive compulsive disorder treatment) as well as the insular cortex (smoking cessation treatment) in addition to the traditional left dorsolateral prefrontal cortex (depression).

The ability to produce a stronger magnetic field allows the stimulation to reach deeper prefrontal neurons and fibers that are more intricately connected to the limbic system (vital deep brain region involved in emotionality, learning, and memory). In the neuroscience literature reviewed in chapter 6, the dorsolateral prefrontal cortex was recognized as a key neuroanatomical mediator of purpose as well as long-term happiness that is achieved through goal striving rather than instant gratification. Thus, it is unsurprising that reduced activation in this region would be a strong marker of depression and subsequently, that providing excitatory stimulation to this area would ameliorate symptoms of depression.[114]

In a large 2019 independent study, the response rate (defined as a 50 percent or higher decrease in depression scores) was significantly greater with Deep TMS (66.7%) than with standard TMS (44.0%). Additionally, remission rates (no longer meeting critical criteria for depression) were 59.7% in the H-coil condition, 41% in the standard TMS condition, and 17% in the control condition.[115]

Both treatments yielded highly encouraging results; however, the 66.7% response rate associated with the Brainsway H-coil represented unprecedented efficacy for the treatment of major depressive disorder. It should be noted that the potential for side effects with TMS are limited but both minor headaches and (very rarely) acute seizures can occur. Acute seizures can arise when the synchronized neural firing produced by the coil persists beyond the TMS train duration.

In a recently published multi-site clinical investigation spanning from 2010 to 2020, 55 documented seizures occurred out of 94,857 patients (.00058% risk).[116] Of the 55 seizure cases, 41 were due to practical errors on the part of the patient or the clinic which included not reporting medication changes, illegal substance abuse, or failure to check motor thresholds at least once every two weeks.[117] Although these incidents are extremely rare and have not lead to any further injuries in the patients, it is important to make patients aware of the potential risk. Notably, there are also well-documented incidents of seizures (.0056% of patients) occurring when psychotropic medications are not administered or taken correctly.[117]

The H-coil from Brainsway recently became the only FDA-approved device for the treatment of OCD (2018), smoking cessation (2021), and anxious depression (2022).

Roughly 60% of patients experiencing depression will also cope with symptoms of anxiety due to a similar neuroanatomical origin. For cases of anxious depression, the Brainsway H1 treatment is still highly effective, yielding a similarly large effect size.[118] The efficacy of the OCD treatment has been assessed using the Yale-Brown Obsessive Compulsive Scale (Y-BOCS), a 10-item checklist scored on a 4-point scale spanning from 0 "no symptoms" to 4 "extreme symptoms". The sum of the first five items is a severity index for obsessions, and the sum of the last five is an index for compulsions. A total score of 0-7 indicates subclinical levels of OCD, while 8-15 denotes mild symptoms, 16-23 signals moderate symptoms, 24-31 indicates severe symptoms, and 32 and up represents extreme levels of OCD.

The 2019 multicenter, double-bind study found that 38.1% of patients in the treatment group achieved a full response reduction (>30% reduction in Y-BOCS score) in symptom severity, compared to just 11.1% in the sham group. Additionally, 54.8% of patients in the active group achieved a partial response of reduction in symptom severity (> 20% reduction in Y-BOCS scores), versus just 26.7% in the sham group.[119] According to the World Health Organization, OCD is one of the top 10 most burdensome and debilitating conditions (mental or physical) known to the world. I have worked with a client that needed to check the closure of their garage door exactly 23 times before leaving the house and another that washed their hands at least 30 times a day to avoid intrusive thoughts about contamination. This condition can be extremely demoralizing and time-consuming, sometimes leaving a person confined to their own home. It also seems to affect a disproportionate number of people who are kind, caring, and conscientious.

Clinically, a 20 or 30 percent reduction in OCD symptoms can represent the fine-line between a patient being unable to leave the house versus regaining their life back through means of socializing with others or obtaining employment opportunities. This is a notoriously difficult condition to treat, in part due to the complex neurocircuitry involving the cortico-striato-thalamo-cortical (CSTC) loop. In the deep TMS treatment of OCD, the treating provider must first provoke a patient so that they fixate on one of their obsessions, thus activating an excitatory signal from the striatum to the cortex by way of the thalamus.

This provocation could include asking the patient to touch a door handle without hand washing, to think about whether they have shut off all of the lights in their home, or even to reflect on a social conversation from the previous day and whether they said "all of the right things". The treatment itself stimulates the inhibitory signal from the frontal cortex back to the striatum which effectively suppresses the obsessional signal from the striatum (to check on something), thus breaking the OCD loop. In healthy individuals, this inhibitory signal is naturally strong enough to suppress obsessional thoughts and allow someone to ease their anxieties by only checking that all the lights are turned off just once.

In OCD, this inhibitory signal is insufficient, allowing the obsessional signal from the striatum to fire in a continuous loop without inhibition or suppression. Therefore, a person can check the lights 20 or 30 times before leaving their house and experience only minimal long-term relief from this obsession.

Tobacco smoking represents one of the leading causes of preventable diseases and fatalities in the U.S. with approximately 34 million U.S. adults smoking cigarettes and roughly 480,000 cigarette-related deaths per year. Smoking addiction has greater prevalence in those with psychiatric ailments and is traditionally one of the most challenging addictions to vanquish. In a 2021 multicenter, double-blind investigation the Deep TMS treatment for smoking cessation was administered in a sample that on average had been smoking for 26 years with no relief from other treatments.

The results demonstrated that for those participants that completed treatment, there was a continuous quit rate (four consecutive weeks of abstinence) of 28.0% in the Deep TMS treatment group compared to 11.7% in the sham condition.[120] Abstinence was verified through weekly urine analysis. This treatment also entails a provocation where craving for cigarettes is induced by way of videos or mental imagery, followed by stimulation of the insular cortex (a region critically involved in addictions).

Additional Deep TMS configurations are currently underway for the treatment of Alzheimer's, Parkinson's, autism spectrum disorder, ADHD, multiple sclerosis, and post-stoke recovery. TMS will likely continue to become more prevalent and serve as a vitally important treatment option in the future of psychiatry as well as neuropsychology, especially with the rising age of the population and the pronounced prevalence of Alzheimer's disease.

Talk Therapy Options

A very common treatment approach aims at targeting the internalization of one's living environment as well as their social experiences via talk therapy. When a person is dealing with a chronic depression episode or existential crisis this will require the support of a professional, providing a sound board for empathetic listening as well as useful cognitive and psychoanalytical coping tools. Numerous forms of evidence-based talk therapies have emerged, most commonly in the form of cognitive behavioral therapy, psychotherapy, and dialectic behavioral therapy. These approaches have yielded comparable efficacy to antidepressant medication when treating mood disorders.[121] Talk therapy has shown to be useful for improving self-esteem, reducing shame and guilt surrounding diagnosis, and for coping with future stress.

Logotherapy, which was developed and outlined by Dr. Viktor Frankl, is one of the few forms of talk therapy that directly aims at training and influencing one's meaning and purpose in life. Frankl began lecturing on a meaning-based form of psychological therapy in the early 1920's, around the same time that he established several youth counseling centers in Vienna, providing free counseling to troubled adolescents.

Due to this initiation, he garnered international attention and had regular correspondence with Sigmund Freud and Alfred Adler, two of the prominent founders of psychology and psychoanalysis. In the 1930's, Frankl finished medical school and began working at "Maria

Theresien Schloessl", a Neurological Hospital in Vienna founded by the Nathaniel Rothschild Foundation.

Frankl became the chief doctor of the "Suicidal Pavilion for Women" at the Psychiatric Hospital in Vienna, and for three years he would gain considerable diagnostic experience by attending to approximately 3000 patients per year.

His next endeavor was to open a private psychiatric practice which unfortunately would only exist for three months due to the Nazi annexation of Austria in 1937. He frequently became outspoken against the Nazi infiltration of his country and the pro-Nazi agendas that many therapists idealized at the time. Frankl was forced to adopt the middle name "Israel" and call himself "Fachbehandler" instead of a practicing physician. His office was "aryanized", and as a result his practice was relocated to his parent's home. In the midst of this chaos, in 1939 he published a paper titled *Philosophy and Psychotherapy* where he coined the expression "Existential Analysis," the philosophical foundation of Logotherapy.

In 1940, he admirably let an immigration visa to America expire to avoid deserting his elderly parents, and he also became the Neurology director at Rothschild Hospital, a clinic for Jewish patients. He often made false diagnoses to save many Jewish people from being euthanized for mental illness. In 1941, he began writing a book titled "The Doctor and the Soul" which would connect existential analysis with logotherapy. He would later be forced to destroy the unpublished novel by Nazi authorities.

Later that year he married Tilly Grosser, a nurse at the Rothschild Hospital and the two became pregnant; however, Nazi authorities would eventually force the couple to have their child aborted. In 1942, Viktor and Tilly were arrested and together with Frankl's parents were deported to the Terezin Ghetto, north of Prague. Later that year, Frankl organized a first response team to provide psychological support to the shocked new arrivals of Terezin camp. In his efforts to protect the inmates from suicide, he was joined by fellow inmate Regina Jonas, the world's first female rabbi.

In 1944, Viktor and Tilly as well as his 65-year-old mother, were transported to the Auschwitz-Birkenau concentration camp. His mother was immediately murdered in a gas chamber. After a few days, Frankl was selected and transferred to a labor camp. He was brought to Kaufering and later Tuerkheim, subsidiary camps of Dachau in Bavaria where he would contract a terrible case of typhoid fever. To avoid a fatal vascular collapse, he would stay up all night, rewriting "The Doctor and the Soul" using stolen paper from the camp office.

In 1945, the camp was finally liberated and within the span of a few days Frankl discovered the deaths of his wife, mother, and brother in Auschwitz. After recovering and finishing his novel in 1945, he would publish the full-length manuscript in 1946 when he also became the director of the Vienna Neurological Policinic (a position he would hold for 25 years). Finally, over the course of nine days (in 1946) he wrote the timeless and inspirational novel *Man's Search for Meaning* which combines his perspective on existentialism, meaning and purpose, and logotherapy with a detailed account of his experience in the concentration camps.

Frankl spent the rest of his life teaching and publishing on the lessons and principles he learned during the most unimaginable circumstances: that people can, and must, find meaning in their lives, even if all they know in their day-to-day life is tremendous suffering. The core of Frankl's philosophy is that a person's deepest desire is to find meaning and purpose in their life, and if that is achieved, then any dream is possible and any circumstance surmountable. Frankl found meaning in his experiences in the concentration camp by deciding that he was going to use his suffering as an opportunity for self-growth. It is nearly impossible to fathom the courage and psychological strength that Frankl championed in order to maintain this mindset.

Instead of becoming apathetic and accepting that he was doomed, he chose to embrace his suffering. According to Frankl, "while a man's destiny in life is certainly affected by the circumstances in which he finds himself, he is ultimately free to choose his own path in life. Even in the worst situation possible, man always has the freedom to choose his attitude towards life." Frankl's perception was that those individuals in the concentration camp that did not experience apathy or "emotional despair" but rather intensified their focus on meaning were the ones that ultimately had a better chance of survival.[7]

Frankl explained that his survival was not based on pure luck and instead it was his "will to meaning" (the desire to live a meaningful life) that allowed him to survive in some of the most horrific and unconceivable circumstances the world has ever seen. Despite the unpredictable dynamic of the concentration camps, those individuals that could stay healthy physically and (especially mentally) had a higher propensity of being spared for work tasks and ultimately surviving. Modern literature has pointed to a highly important link between perceived purpose and health outcomes, providing support to Dr.

Treatment Options

Frankl's conclusion about his survival not being due to pure luck of the draw.

Frankl explained that three overarching sources of meaning allowed him to maintain his spirits during the holocaust; these include his work (the desire to one day publish a novel on logotherapy), his love (to his fiancé that tragically passed away although he did not know this at the time), and his commitment to suffering. The latter may come as a surprise to some, but just as there is beauty in overcoming long-term obstacles there can be great meaning, knowledge, and self-awareness obtained through perseverance of suffering. Frankl posited the term "super meaning" which is used to refer to themes of meaning and answers to questions that are out of reach when it comes to our human mental and spiritual capacity. Instead of spending endless time dwelling on these answers Frankl advises us to find ways that make each individual moment valuable.[7]

What finally snapped my 22-year-old self out of existential crisis and towards an existence full of drive and joy towards living life was the realization that the most purposeful life was that which could be spent maximizing each and every moment. In-line with the teachings of logotherapy, if one can give their full attention and purpose to each individual moment then existential frustration or crisis can be averted. Frankl also held the belief (which I have echoed here) that each person has a unique vocation where a flow can be reached, and they are "clicking on all cylinders" as a spirit. He explains that man's "will to meaning" can become existentially frustrated, which can in turn provoke "noögenic neuroses".

In other words, if a man cannot find the meaning or purpose in his life, he can develop mental problems that need to be addressed. Frankl argues that everyone should strive to be in a state of "noö-dynamics", in which there is a tension between what one has already done and what one hopes to accomplish. Only then can a person maintain a hunger and goal-oriented approach to living their life. Those individuals with existential crises or neuroses may require logotherapy to aid them in the path to purpose.

Man's Search for Meaning also introduces the concept of paradoxical intention; a cognitive technique that consists of persuading or tricking a patient to engage in his or her most feared behavior. This technique is broadly used to treat insomnia, anxiety, specific phobias and obsessive-compulsive tendencies. For example, if a patient is terrified of falling asleep a therapist may instruct them to try and stay awake throughout the whole night; thus, diminishing performance anxiety related to the issue.

If discomfort is largely related to internal factors associated with anxiety, then paradoxical intention is an excellent treatment of choice. A characteristic complaint could be "I am afraid that when giving a public speech, I will become very anxious and my heart rate will spike to the point that I will lose control, become ill, or experience a heart attack." From Frankl's perspective, the core instruction administered to such a client should be to focus on manifesting the most salient aspect of sympathetic activity during the presentation; basically, "try to increase your heart rate as much as possible."

I recently worked with a client struggling with social anxiety and hyperhidrosis. The client reported that the more anxious they felt about their excessive sweating and the harder they tried to make it stop, it only would become more intense. Using the paradoxical intention technique, I instructed the client to focus on creating as much sweat and perspiration as possible when speaking to someone, especially a person they deemed as attractive or likeable. The client initially laughed at this idea but steadily began committing to the approach and reporting fewer and fewer incidents of hyperhidrosis. The patient also reported feeling a tremendous calm and lightness once they realized that they no longer had to "battle" the issue but instead could defeat this demon in an easier manner.

Logotheory

Frankl's theory of logotherapy, entitled "logotheory", provides a framework of connection between concepts such as "will-to-meaning", "existential frustration", "existential vacuum", "will-to-pleasure", "will-to-power", and "noogenic" neurosis. Frankl (1984) proposed that the "will-to-meaning", or the intense desire to discover the unique meaning and purpose to one's life, is the primary motivation in human beings. The "will-to-meaning" serves as a guiding force in all circumstances of a person's life, pushing them to discover sense, purpose, and meaning in days, hours, and even minutes. From a developmental psychology perspective, this innate force occurs across the lifespan.

When meaning is achieved it sort of connects a person's sense of self to the people, social environment, and circumstances that they interact with. This connectedness and coherence provide an existential energy and optimism that enables the psychological perception of direction and purpose. Life circumstances and problematic behaviors can interfere with the "will-to-meaning" and make it difficult for an individual to attain a sense of meaning and purpose, causing "existential frustration", or a state of "discouraged will-to-meaning".[122] The "existential vacuum" or an inner experience of emptiness or purposelessness, occurs because of "existential frustration". Furthermore, Frankl believed that existential frustration and the subsequent vacuum are closely intertwined or caused by the "will-to-pleasure" and the "will-to-power", which are two alternative guiding forces of human behavior, that are less positively influential and can be difficult to distinguish from the "will-to-meaning".

The "will-to-pleasure" manifests in an unrestrained pursuit of hedonistic pleasure, such as sexual obsession or drug addiction, and the "will-to-power" contributes to preoccupation with social status, money, or material items along with displays of social aggression and antisocial behaviors. Because contemporary western culture emphasizes materialism and embraces immediate gratification, it is not uncommon for people to unknowingly have the "will-to-meaning" thwarted by the "will-to pleasure" and the "will-to-power". The pursuit of material items absorbs time and energy, and as Frankl suggested, the search for meaning likely becomes entangled with such pursuits, making it difficult to discern these three constructs.

Prolonged fixation with the "will-to-pleasure" and the "will-to-power" will interfere with the achievement of "will-to-meaning", thus increasing the likelihood of "existential vacuum". A vicious cycle can then occur as people may further strive for the "will-to-pleasure" and the "will-to-power" in the hopes of filling voids of emptiness within their life, that can only truly be cemented with the "will-to-meaning".

Lastly, "noogenic neurosis" can occur which as a pathology can be conceptualized as a spiritual sickness.

Frankl believed "noogenic neurosis" to be purely existential but highly related to issues of psychopathology (e.g., depression, anxiety, or obsessive–compulsive disorder). Frankl emphasized that the specific causes of "noogenic neuroses" are highly variant and that overexposure to "existential vacuum" and "existential frustration" may contribute to its emergence and that deficits in psychological well-being occur when these cycles of purposelessness intensify. The primary role of the logotherapist is to determine whether a patient is suffering an existential crisis and help them in the process of uncovering the source of "noogenic neurosis" whether it be a lack of "will-to-meaning" or an overemphasis of "will-to-pleasure". The therapist and client then work on strategies for once again striving towards meaning and purpose in life.

Today, logotherapy is not practiced, utilized, or researched to the extent of CBT, DBT, or psychotherapy; however, there are centers in Texas, Arizona, Canada, Mexico, South Africa Israel, Australia, Ireland, Finland, Argentina, and Brazil that practice this approach. The existing research on this therapy supports positive results, often with mid-to-large effect sizes. A recent meta-analysis (multi-study compilation) on 6 randomized control trials (RCTs) with one group receiving logotherapy treatments found large effects of the treatment on positive meaning in life immediately post-intervention, as well as on psychopathology and self-efficacy.[123]

Another meta-analysis was conducted on 10 controlled trials of logotherapy (6 randomized and 4 nonrandomized) featuring 623 patients with cancer. The therapeutic effects were compared with usual care control groups or other psychosocial interventions. Across all studies, the effect size of the treatment was large for improved meaning in life and was moderate for improved spiritual well-being and quality of life as well as reduced anxiety and physical discomfort.[124]

Spiritually sensitive psychotherapy (an Islamic form of logotherapy) was utilized in a treatment study that was conducted with university students in Iran. Sixty university students with elevated depression symptoms at baseline were randomly assigned to either a twelve-session group logotherapy program or a control group.

Results showed that spiritually sensitive logotherapy significantly reduced depression, anxiety, and stress, relative to the control group (with a large effect size).[125] Logotherapy interventions have also proven beneficial in reducing stress amongst multiple sclerosis patients and are being infused into both family-dynamic and elderly-care therapeutic models with greater regularity.

Logotherapy Application for Modern Times

Many psychologists, philosophers, and sociologists have acutely observed a global shift in the human social experience as a result of the technological revolution of the past 20-30 years. With the introduction of the laptop, iPad, iPhone, Nintendo DS, and Android, the human race has directed their attention span further into the screen and less on the environment around them, which includes direct social engagement. These inventions have tremendous benefits on civilization in terms of allowing information sharing, remote communication opportunities with close others, as well as new opportunities for game play and excitement.

However, it is very possible that the technological revolution has occurred too rapidly and that countless individuals are now missing out on essential time spent in nature and engaged in meaningful face-to-face interactions with others. Rates of depression, anxiety, OCD, and suicide are at higher levels than ever previously recorded in civilization. All the while reported life-satisfaction and purpose in life are also lower as evidenced by results on the long withstanding General Social Survey. Between 1990 and 2018 the number of people in the United States reporting that they are "not too happy" increased from 8 to 13 percent.[126]

It could be said that we are living in a society that has everything and yet nothing at the same time. Additionally, algorithms on YouTube, Instagram, and Facebook have become clever enough to feed us a continuous stream of videos, reels, or images that capture our own unique interests. From a neurophysiological perspective, this leads to a spike in dopamine production as we are watching this content of choice. Unfortunately, given the continuous and instant nature of this content, pausing the video, and putting away the phone will eventually disrupt dopamine production to a point that initiates physical sensations of pain.

As a consequence, it may become more and more difficult for people to become excitable to traditional stimulation occurring outside of the screen whether its interacting with family or a romantic partner, playing sports, running, eating, or petting a puppy. Although technological advancements have allowed us to connect with anyone across the globe, complete master's degrees from the comfort of our living room, and even obtain endless access to long-forgotten songs from the 80's, these advancements have also guided people further and further into the "will-to-pleasure" via instant gratification.

When continually reinforced, the "will-to-pleasure" culminates into the "existential vacuum" (frustration) and potential "noogenic neurosis". The use of cellular devices and social media does not effectively guide an individual towards the "will-to-meaning"; instead, it pulls them further and further from reality, where purpose is ultimately achieved. Dr. Frankl's theory is nearly a hundred years old, but its principles provide us with a highly useful framework for understanding the current mental health epidemic that has occurred so rapidly it cannot simply be explained by increased awareness on the topic.

Increased awareness related to mental health has occurred and is highly beneficial for society as it will enable 1) more and more individuals to seek out mental health management options due to de-stigmatization 2) increased research and implementation of cutting-edge treatment options and 3) a shift towards a positive psychological perspective where mental health is viewed as something that can be trained and strengthened on a continuum rather than an "all or nothing" approach.

Increased Purpose Through Expansion of the Mind

A well-known phenomenon in research on human performance is "flow",[127] defined as a state of full-task engagement corresponding with low levels of self-referential thinking (e.g., worrying, self-reflection). Flow is often associated with athletes, artists, or musicians who are fully absorbed in a task and able to achieve peak performance. However, flow-like states can also occur in day-to-day situations, like a burst of creativity experienced during a morning run or when a nurse is so engaged with their patients that they lose track of time.

The experience of flow is often accompanied by a sense of accomplishment, meaningfulness, and positive mood states. Achieving a "flow" state of physiology has a major role in well-being. It has been established that, in order to experience flow, a key criterion is the alignment between the difficulty of the task and a person's abilities to complete that task. Should a task be too easy or routine it may lead to boredom and lack of sustained attention, rather than flow. A task that is overchallenging will often lead to frustration and stress which are typically incompatible with achieving a flow state. People who reported experiencing high levels of flow retroactively in their life, also reported feeling in control, having a clear sense of direction (i.e., clear goals), and a condensed perception of time.[127] A condensed perception of time during the workday is a highly appealing thought to many.

The locus coeruleus (LC) is a nucleus within the pons (brain stem) section of the brain that is largely responsible for regulating levels of norepinephrine (NE) within the central nervous system. Thus, it has a broad influence on the arousal levels in the brain and interacts with many distinct regions including the hippocampus and ventral tegmental area. Although the primary function of the LC-NE system is regulating arousal levels, some neuroscientists have theorized that it is also involved with more complex functions.[128]

The LC-NE system seems to exert an influence on the decision to focus versus disengage on specific tasks, and making an evaluation of whether energy or arousal is warranted given the reward of successfully completing the task. If a suitable reward is interpreted, the LC-NE system facilitates a brain state supporting task-relevant information processing, while inhibiting task-irrelevant stimuli. However, if the costs of the effort outweigh the perceived benefits, the LC-NE system changes its activity in a way that makes task engagement more arduous and there will be a greater likelihood of distractibility. The tendency to lock-in on a task is referred to as "exploitation", and the distractibility or desire to find a more suitable task is "exploration".[128]

A recent study[129] investigated the electrophysiology of "flow" using (EEG) measures that were tied to the execution of a mental arithmetic task in a total of 16 participants (10 males, 6 females). Self-reported perceptions of task-induced flow state were measured along with EEG metrics across three different conditions (Boredom, Flow, and Overload) that were named based on task difficulty. As anticipated, subjective ratings of "flow perception" indicated the highest levels of flow in the flow condition.

Regarding the EEG data, theta activity in the frontal cortex was higher in both the flow and the overload conditions compared to the boredom condition. Alpha activity in the frontal areas and the right midline region was also gradually increased as task difficulty was raised. These EEG band activity patterns correlated with self-reported flow experience, especially items related to concentration on the task and task difficulty.

This finding is in-line with the previous literature on EEG frequency waves which broadly characterizes the alpha wave as indicating an optimal calm, yet focused state where the brain can achieve peak creativity, while theta is prominent during internal focus, meditation, prayer, and spiritual awareness. Theta reflects the state between wakefulness and sleep, and relates to the subconscious mind as evidenced by its high prevalence during rapid-eye movement sleep[129], where most subconscious-influenced dreaming takes place.

Eye movement desensitization and reprocessing or EMDR, is a form of psychotherapy developed by Francine Shapiro in the 1980s for treating PTSD via communication with the subconscious mind. This therapy is believed to guide the brain into a theta activation state, although it has not yet been tested empirically. Increased theta activation could also potentially explain why individuals in a flow state often report being unaware of the passing of time.

Given the link between a state of flow and increased purpose or meaning it would be prudent to utilize treatment or training approaches that promote the theta and alpha state. From a training perspective, meditative exercises have shown to positively promote both of these activity states. Transcendental meditation (a 15-20-minute daily practice involving attention to a silent mantra) is an approach that yields significant increases in alpha and theta power (amount of activity) as well as alpha coherence (synchronization of brain regions within this activity state).[131]

Other forms of meditation including mindfulness meditation, spiritual meditation, progressive relaxation, and loving-kindness meditation have produced positive results in promoting these brain activity states as well as leading to reduced issues of internalization disorders. Mindfulness meditation is the practice of being present in the moment and allowing the mind to wander without any judgement or redirection. It is simply the practice of openly monitoring one's thoughts, one's breathing, and one's physiology for an extended period. I have observed first-hand how mindfulness meditation can have positive effects on emotional well-being and relevant brain activation patterns. In a recent study[132] we observed the effects of a 10-week mindfulness meditation intervention conducted for children in several elementary school classrooms.

The participants (7-10-year-olds) reported significantly reduced traits of anxiety and depression, and demonstrated increases in interhemispheric alpha coherence, as well as increased theta, alpha, and beta power particularly in frontal and central areas. These alterations reflect a lowered neurophysiological risk for the development of mood disorders throughout adolescence and adulthood. Given the plasticity of the adolescent brain, it is highly important for positive mental health practices to be taught to children around the world at a young age. The work being done by Mindful Powers and Smiling Mind to make meditation practice and knowledge accessible and kid-friendly is commendable.

In another study[133] our team replicated the 10-week program in a sample of school-aged participants (9-11-years-old) and improvements in creativity were also identified. We also found that students scoring lower on baseline creativity and attention measures were more likely to report unfavorable experiences with regards to mindfulness; however, they were also more likely to report greater reductions in depression from baseline to post-treatment.

This illustrates that despite meditation practices not feeling pleasurable or coming easily to these children, they still reaped strong benefits from having the practice incorporated into their daily classroom experience. Personally, I have learned to become a better meditator over the years and have admiration and appreciation for its importance, but had I been asked whether I enjoy it as a 22-year-old or especially a 10-year-old, the answer would have been a resounding no. It is probably the case that the individuals that are most resistant to meditation (myself included) would experience the most profound benefit from this exercise.

Since having a qEEG brain scan conducted on myself in 2019, I learned that I needed to use more tools to recover from stress and anxiety. As a result, I have tried to implement daily meditation and breathing exercises (box breathing or Wim Hoff Breathing), and my scan in 2022 appears much improved and more importantly, so is my quality of life.

Meditation with Performance Feedback

In the 1960's Dr. Barry Sterman a renowned professor at UCLA, would often conduct behavioral experiments with his cats in order to teach them a variety of new tricks and behaviors. One day he sought to determine whether the same type of reinforcements (operant conditioning) could actually be used to impact the way that the cat's brains were operating. Amazingly, the cats were able to successfully increase the time spent with their brain activity locked into a 12-15 Hz range when they were rewarded with food.

A few years later, Dr. Sterman was doing an experiment for NASA on whether rocket fuel causes seizures and he used the same cats as experiment subjects. During this study he found (to his great surprise) that the cats who had undergone the brain activity training were significantly less likely to experience seizures than other cats. Dr. Sterman would later apply this technique to humans suffering from epilepsy, where he found that following several weeks of training, 60% of the subjects were able to reduce their epileptic seizures by 20-100%, and that the results were long lasting.

Around the same time, Dr. Joe Kamiya discovered that through the use of operant conditioning humans could learn to gain control of their brain waves to maximize focus and creativity. He trained people to achieve an alpha state by rewarding them with the sound of a bell. Dr. Barry Sterman and Dr. Joe Kamiya conducted the first examples of delivering real-time feedback to humans based on the second-by-second brain activity traits they were displaying (measured via EEG electrodes). These were the first instances of what would later be referred to as **neurofeedback training**.

In 1968, Dr. Kamiya published a paper in Psychology Today on this technique that caught the attention of Dr. Joel Lubar (a professor at the University of Chicago). Dr. Lubar would go onto apply the practice of neurofeedback to treating attention deficit hyperactivity disorder (ADHD) in children, adolescents, and adults. He published dozens of randomized control studies in the 1970's that validated neurofeedback as an effective tool for improving sustained attention and impulsivity in individuals with ADHD.

Since then, a significant body of research on the efficacy of neurofeedback therapy for the treatment of ADHD has emerged, with many studies showing significant and long-term improvements on hyperactivity, inattention, and impulsivity after neurofeedback treatment.[134] This technology is also used by many practices to treat mood disorders, help prevent cognitive decline in neurological conditions like Alzheimer's, and to maximize day-to-day cognitive performance in professionals, athletes, and musicians.[135]

With modern technology, neurofeedback involves the simultaneous occurrence of two events: 1) the continuous recording of one's brain activity in a targeted area (e.g. right parietal cortex or P4) in a second-by-second resolution and 2) feedback provided to the participant through a software that informs them how successfully their brain is regulating to the targeted brain wave frequency (e.g., alpha or 8 to 12 Hz).

The feedback can be provided to an individual in a myriad of ways. In a more basic form of training, a user can watch a bar that turns green every time their brain hits the alpha state, or red every time they fall outside of this range and back into counterproductive activation states. The objective would be for the user to just focus on keeping the bar green for as long as possible and when the goal-directed behavior is set with full intention, the brain is miraculous in its ability to modify its activation state based on feedback from the environment. Using newer and more advanced neurofeedback software, activity measurements can be linked to a game (e.g. a pacman character moving on screen and accumulating points when activity is in range and slowing down when activity shifts out of range) or the playing of a movie (e.g. Step Brothers will play fluidly when activity is in range and freeze when a user gets out of range.)

The trick is to find the suitable reinforcement that will keep the participant engaged and motivated to improve their scores and effectively rewire their brain. If a user pays attention to the screen and has the desire and intention to improve, the brain will properly regulate its activity to solve the problem and earn the reward. One of my clients adequately described neurofeedback as "meditation where you get to see how well you are actually doing". Other clients have described neurofeedback as "strength and resistance training for the brain" and even a "brain marathon".

Neurofeedback training of alpha and theta activation states was implemented by Eugene Peniston of the V.A. Medical Center of Fort Lyon, Colorado for the treatment of Vietnam veterans with PTSD. Peniston's aim was to reduce depression and anxiety and restore motivation and purpose in these veterans. The MMPI (Multiphasic Personality Inventory) was used pre-training and again after the 30-day program. The group given 30 sessions of 30-minute alpha-theta training had significant reductions in many domains of the MMPI including hypochondriasis, depression, hysteria, psychopathic, deviate, paranoia, schizophrenia, hypomania, and social introversion compared to the treatment as usual (TAU) group that was given antipsychotic medication with group therapy. A thirty-month follow-up showed that only three of the 15 neurofeedback participants had regressed.[136]

In a follow-up study the researchers found that the same protocol led to significant reductions in alcohol consumption in 14 alcoholic patients, an effect that was sustained at a 21-month follow-up assessment.[137] Although this protocol has not been directly assessed for maximizing the neurophysiological "flow state"; there have been numerous recent evaluations of its utility for athletes and musicians attempting to reach peak performance and heightened purpose.

In a meta-analysis that included 10 randomized controlled trials aimed to assess the effect of neurofeedback training on sport performance in athletes, significant effects of neurofeedback were found for sport performance across a variety of different demands. The sports included in the analysis were golf putting, shooting, dance, gymnastics and swimming.[138] Other case studies have shown that the enhancement of the alpha wave provides benefits on creativity and performance measures for actors, musicians, and dancers.[139]

Promoting Brain Changes Through Psychedelics

In the 1950s, a well-known Swiss pharmaceutical company named Sandoz, began making psychedelic drugs available to the psychiatric research community. Albert Hofmann, the lead chemist at the time, was the first known person to isolate, synthesize, and name lysergic acid diethylamide (LSD) as well as the similar serotonergic compounds psilocybin and psilocin, commonly known as "magic mushrooms". These drugs were produced and distributed to psychiatric practices under the product names Delysid and Indocybin, respectively.

For the next 15 years, these drugs revolutionized neuropsychiatry because of their frequent use by researchers and clinicians in many countries, including the US. Unbeknownst to many, there were over 100 empirical investigations on the utility of LSD and Psilocybin which showed positive effects on a range of clinical symptoms including addiction, anxiety, depression, and PTSD.

Due to the popularity of these drugs for recreational abuse as well as an association with anti-Vietnam war protests, they would be banned in the U.S. in the late 1960's and the rest of the world would follow in 1971. Due to this global ban, manufacturing of medical-grade psychedelics became virtually eliminated and obtaining IRB approval or funding for research projects became an extremely difficult process.

Treatment Options

There has recently been a revolution of research on the application of medical-grade psychedelics in a controlled, clinical setting for participants with a variety of psychiatric issues. Certain studies have also been conducted with healthy volunteers hoping to advance our understanding of the precise mechanisms by which psychedelics influence consciousness and neurocircuitry (and also probably to experience an incredible high).

The Johns Hopkins University Center for Psychedelic and Consciousness Research has spearheaded this movement since year 2000, when they became the first research organization to obtain regulatory approval in the US to reinstate psychedelic research with healthy, psychedelic-naïve volunteer participants.

Johns Hopkins is particularly interested in the potential of psychedelic treatments to precipitate profound mystical experiences in everyday humans that are sometimes reported as "mind-altering and life-changing". A compilation of recent research from this lab has effectively highlighted the potential of these substances for helping individuals to overcome severe and treatment-resistant depression, cope with trauma, overcome addictions, and find greater purpose and connection with the world around them.

In 2014, the lab reported results from a sample of 200 volunteers, each of whom received at least one daylong session (approximately 12 hours) involving a large dose of psilocybin (3 to 4 grams). Roughly two-thirds of the volunteers ranked their session as one of the most meaningful experiences of their lives and reported that they experienced positive changes in their mood, behaviors, and overall well-being as days and weeks passed.[140] The volunteers were characterized as both psychologically and physically healthy and possessing some spiritual interest but having no prior experience taking psychedelics before.

Notably, some of the 200 participants were chronic tobacco smokers, trying to achieve cessation through this alternative option, and others were cancer patients seeking relief from psychological distress occurring as a result of their diagnosis.

In the lab's initial study back in 2006, the researchers were intrigued by the anecdotes they received from volunteers after the sessions, with regards to levels of profoundness and spiritual meaning perceived from the experience. To capture these responses, they added two questions asking volunteers to rate on a multipoint scale how "personally meaningful" and how "spiritually significant" their sessions were. The top two rating options for both of these items were "among the top five of my life" and "the single most of my life."

In the data collected on these two Likert-scaled items two months after the psilocybin session, approximately 65 percent of the sample reported that the experience was "among the top five of their life" from either a personally meaningful or spiritual perspective. For an experience to be considered as "top 5 throughout life" it would be perceived as on-par with other events like graduating college, experiencing a first kiss, getting married, having a child, and perhaps trying spaghetti carbonara for the first time.[141]

A whopping one-third of the volunteers rated the session as the single most spiritually significant experience of their lives. When they were asked again at a 14-month follow-up, the volunteer ratings of the experience were not significantly altered. From a psychiatric perspective, it is astonishing that a session involving a single dose of a drug could preface such a sustained response. As always, it is important to determine how much of the effects were due to the psilocybin versus the magnitude of a placebo effect, possibly caused by the overall experience of an all-day event which allowed participants a chance to relax, listen to music of their choosing, and turn completely inward.

Although volunteers provided positive ratings of the personal meaning and spiritual significance for sessions in which they received the control drug (methylphenidate), none of these sessions were rated as either the most "personally meaningful" or the most "spiritually significant" of a lifetime. Further, none of the participants in the psilocybin condition rated the experience as "not meaningful at all" compared to 10 percent of the methylphenidate condition.[141]

Another investigation in 2011 examined the impact of treatment dose and showed that the perceptions of meaning and spiritual significance increase as a function of the dose. In this investigation, volunteers received five total sessions, one of which was a placebo session and four were psilocybin sessions, one low dose, one medium dose, one medium-high dose, and a high dose. The researchers surveyed the volunteers one month after each of the sessions and found that higher doses had a greater likelihood of leading to perception of a profound experience. Ninety-four percent of the volunteers rated at least one session as amongst the top-five "personally meaningful" or top-five "spiritually significant" events of their lives.[142]

Treatment Options

At a 14-month follow-up investigation, 83 percent of the 200 participants reported that life satisfaction was increased "moderately" or "very much", and 90 percent reported "moderate" or "more positive behavior change", with 44 percent reporting the change as "strong" or "extreme." To further cover all bases, the researchers obtained contact information for three individuals that were close to the participant and could be surveyed regarding changes in behavior or mindset because of the treatment.

Telephone interviews were conducted with these individuals close to the time of enrollment, one month after the last session, and at a 14-month follow-up. In each interview the close observers were asked to rate the volunteer on an 11-item questionnaire. The items captured were inner peace, patience, playfulness, mental flexibility, optimism, anxiety, interpersonal perceptiveness, expression of anger, compassion/social concern, expression of positive emotions, and self-confidence. The scores on all item measures were significantly improved at 1-month and 14-month follow-up based on the reports.[143]Additional research from this team found that ratings of spiritual significance at the 14-month follow-up were more heavily predicted by self-reported mysticism scores immediately after the session rather than perceptions of "how intense the effects of the drug were". Mystical experiences are defined differently throughout the world but can be broadly conceptualized as an uncommon occurrence when an individual feels heightened connection to a person, to God, or the world in general. These experiences are considered to be psychologically healthy and full of meaning and purpose.

Treatment Options

A common concern that both volunteers and especially patients present with in regard to psychedelics is the potential for disassociation, fear, anxiety, and paranoia. These concerns highlight the importance of delivering these treatments in a clinical setting through a controlled dose, and with a well-trained team of professionals closely monitoring the individuals receiving the dose. The lab at Johns Hopkins also collected data indicating the likelihood for these various side effects to occur.

In the initial study, 33 percent of volunteers reported strong or extreme ratings of fear after receiving psilocybin; however, none reported this after receiving methylphenidate. Intervals of fear or anxiety had unpredictable times of onset and durations during the session.[141] In the 2011 study, this challenging reaction occurred in 39 percent of volunteers, primarily at the highest dose and with only one incident occurring from the medium-high dose. The authors concluded that there may be a "sweet spot" between the two doses highlighting a zone where maximum meaning can be perceived but with a mitigated risk of side-effects.[142]

Following the promising results of these studies on a sample of healthy volunteers, the team at Johns Hopkins has also conducted several clinical trials for both depression and addictions. A 2022 study consisting of 24 patients aged 21–75 with moderate to severe unipolar depression randomly assigned half the participants to an immediate or delayed (8 weeks) treatment condition in which they were given two full-day treatments (1st dose 20 mg, 2nd dose 30 mg) of psilocybin with corresponding psychotherapy.

Treatment Options

The participants were surveyed for 12 months following the second dose and significant decreases from baseline depression scores were documented at all the follow-up points (1-, 3-, 6-, and 12-month follow-up). At 12 months, the response rate in this sample was 75% (50% reduction of symptoms or more) and the remission rate was 58%, with no serious adverse events being reported.[144]

In a 2014 investigation, 15 chronic cigarette smokers received 2 or 3 doses of psilocybin along with cognitive behavioral therapy for smoking cessation. At 6-month follow-up, 12 of the 15 smokers (80%) demonstrated smoking abstinence (verified biologically). Participants who responded were compared to those that did not quit smoking at 6 months and abstainers scored significantly higher on a measure to gauge perceived mystical experience, however their subjective ratings of the "intensity of the dose" did not differ. Perceptions of the mystical experience also correlated with later reports of personal meaning and spiritual significance suggesting that achieving a mystical experience could play a vital role in overcoming addictions.[145]

A Horse Tranquilizer for Human Healing

Ketamine (often known better by its street name "special K") is commonly used by doctors and veterinarians for the induction and maintenance of anesthesia. It is also the only psychedelic drug that currently has FDA approval (as of 2019) for the treatment of clinical depression, but only when it is delivered in its nasal spray form, known as esketamine. The antidepressant effects of ketamine were first discovered by emergency medical staff that would use the drug to calm patients down after a rescued suicide attempt.

Treatment Options

The anecdotes of these patients experiencing remission from depression in the coming months began to pile up, igniting further research and attention surrounding this drug. Ketamine works differently than traditional antidepressant agents (including SSRI's and psilocybin) as it is believed to regulate glutamate levels within the brain rather than serotonin or dopamine. Glutamate is the most abundant excitatory neurotransmitter produced by the brain and it plays an essential role in both learning new materials and formulating/storing memories.

Researchers and clinicians are still attempting to understand the precise mechanisms by which ketamine has a positive effect on mental health, but one hypothesis suggests the possibility that ketamine causes the blocking of a key glutamate receptor (NMDA receptor), subsequently inhibiting the release of this neurotransmitter and reducing neurological inflammation.[146] Another theory posits that despite blocking NMDA receptors in the post-synaptic cells, ketamine does not block glutamate binding to adjacent AMPA receptors, creating a net gain in AMPA activation and subsequent glutamate production in key neuroanatomical regions.[147] The latter theory would explain the antidepressant effect of ketamine given that glutamate levels are often deficient in this condition.

Lastly, it is believed that ketamine stimulates an expeditious upregulation of BDNF (brain-derived neurotrophic factor) which is a key protein that generates both neurogenesis and synaptogenesis. If this is the case, ketamine would be priming the brain for rapid change to take place, essentially recycling damaged connections in favor of stronger and healthier ones. Interestingly, cerebrospinal fluid investigations of patients with obsessive compulsive disorders have revealed heightened glutamate levels in the plasma, yet ketamine has shown to have powerful anti-obsession effects in addition to anti-depressant. Based on these results it is reasonable to suspect that ketamine regulates glutamate levels in some way (whether they are heightened or deficient) by way of promoting BDNF levels and inducing staggering neuroplasticity.[148]

Ketamine is most effective and works most rapidly when delivered intravenously, intramuscular, or via nasal spray rather than orally. In the typical course of sessions for treatment-resistant depression, patients usually receive the nasal spray or IV twice a week for 1 to 4 weeks; then once a week for weeks 5 to 9; and then once every week or 2 after that. Like psilocybin, ketamine has the potential to cause a dissociative experience that could potentially be mystical depending on how it's perceived by the individual. Aside from the effect of ketamine on the brain (modulation of glutamate and enabling new neural pathways to form), the subjective experience can be highly profound and meaningful to the user.

Some clients I have worked with have reported that they "felt more connected with the world", "felt like they were seeing the world from a different perspective", and even that "they were able to reframe traumatic or troublesome memories from their past" following single sessions of the treatment. However, numerous clients have reported side effects including anxiety, nausea, and fatigue. The two-to-three-hour experience can also raise heart rate and blood pressure, which is why preexisting conditions related to high blood pressure or heart issues are contraindicative for the treatment.

A recent large-scale community investigation (9016 patients) on the efficacy of IV ketamine yielded a 50% response rate and a 30% remission rate, with an overall significant reduction of depressive symptoms and suicide ideation in the sample. The treatment phase was characterized as 4-8 infusions administered over a 7-28-day span.[149] Long-term sustainment of effects was approximately 80% at 4 weeks and 60% at 8 weeks. Intranasal esketamine (provided by Spravato TM) has yielded similar efficacy in reducing depressive symptoms following a 56 MG dose (one spray in each nostril) given twice weekly for 4 weeks, then once weekly for another 4 weeks.

Approximately 65 percent of patients experience an anti-depressant response and 32 percent experience full remission while also taking an antidepressant medication.[150] Ketamine has wide-spread potential for the treatment of other psychiatric conditions including PTSD, OCD, and anxiety. The early findings appear promising and comparable to the efficacy for depression; however further research is necessary and warranted.[151]

It is advantageous to gain a better understanding as to how ketamine affects the brain from a neurophysiological perspective so that the benefits that occur from the profound subjective experience of mysticism can better be better understood and characterized. It is possible that ketamine can tap into the subconscious mind and allow the reframing of traumatic or repressed memories, especially when paired with psychotherapy.

A 2018 investigation from researchers at the University of Hawaii assessed the neurophysiological effects of ketamine using magnetoencephalography (MEG) in 35 subjects with major depressive disorder (MDD) and 25 healthy controls. The study was a randomized cross-over trial consisting of sessions with 0.5 mg/kg of ketamine delivered. MDD subjects showed significant improvements in depressive symptoms and both groups showed increased resting gamma power (> 30 Hz) following infusions. Gamma is the fastest-paced activity produced by the brain; it tends to be dominant when a person is intensively engaged or actively focused in solving a problem.

Baseline levels of gamma power were also found to moderate the effectiveness of ketamine on antidepressant response; specifically, individuals with lower baseline gamma levels had an increased likelihood for antidepressant response along with heightened gamma levels post-ketamine. Those participants with higher levels of baseline gamma were less likely to respond. This study not only highlighted a potential neurophysiological effect of ketamine (heightened gamma activity) but also introduced the possibility that EEG biomarkers could be used for the selection of certain types of antidepressant treatments.[152]

Another study examined the EEG dynamics that occurred during ketamine infusions delivered to 12 sheep (Ovis Aries). Consistent with the findings of Nugent and colleagues, the authors found heightened levels of gamma bursts in the frontal cortex (27-40 Hz) during the infusion. Notably, they also found heightened levels of theta oscillations (4 to 8 Hz) with reduced alpha and beta oscillations.[153] From a physiological perspective, theta dominance along with spontaneous bursts of gamma activity is characteristic of rapid eye movement sleep. Gamma brain waves are especially correlated with problem solving, memory consolidation, and higher states of awareness and attention.

During ketamine treatment, it is possible that the constant calming flow of theta activity (often seen during meditation) primes the brain for a powerful learning experience and the bursts of gamma are representative of the brain reprocessing both old memories and perspectives of the world while gaining new insights.[154] Lastly, one innovative study correlated EEG response to ketamine with subjective ratings of dissociative levels. They found that reduced alpha activity and increased theta were related to higher self-reported disassociation.[155]

The delivery of psychedelic drugs such as ketamine, psilocybin, and LSD by a clinical team represents a very promising tool for the treatment of major depression, suicide ideation, addiction, and existential crisis. It is especially fascinating that a large percentage of participants rate these experiences as amongst the most meaningful of their entire life (in-line with marriage and the birth of a child). However, there are some serious side effects that can occur and not all patients report the experience as positive, some perceive fear, panic, and dissociation.

Notably, many of the other approaches discussed earlier in the book (yoga, meditation, neurofeedback, logotherapy) are capable of invoking the theta activation state that occurs under the influence of ketamine. These alternative treatment options also have the potential to facilitate purpose and mysticism on a more day-to-day basis and with fewer side effects than psychedelics. Overall, I feel that this treatment tool is best-utilized when a person is dealing with clinical,

Treatment Options

treatment-resistant conditions and not as a first-line approach to assisting with mental illness or existential crises. Hopefully, this perspective will not be lost as psychedelics continue to gain traction in the field of neuroscience, psychopharmacology, and popular culture at large. These powerful drugs have great potential but as history has taught us, must be used with care and control.

Closing Thoughts

It is my profound hope that this book will be useful to individuals who care about pursuing a greater purpose in life as well as those who have experienced the deep despair of an existential crisis. From my professional and personal opinion, finding purpose in life is essential for well-being and longevity, life-satisfaction and happiness, and spiritual enlightenment. However, finding purpose in a constantly evolving world that does not come with a manual can be one of life's greatest challenges. It is also extremely exhilarating, and committing to the pursuit of purpose is the most worthwhile journey a person can take.

Viktor Frankl and other proponents of logotherapy believe that instilled within the core of our very being and spirit is a deep desire to find this purpose and more importantly to strive for it on a daily basis. My hope is that these chapters will help to renew a philosophical perspective that is too often underappreciated in a modern world that places more and more value on instant gratification, hedonistic pleasures, and material goods. Living merely to obtain these worldly objectives frequently leads to feelings of emptiness, despair, and existential crisis. In contrast, when someone is able to immerse themselves within a task, objective, study, hobby, activity, or gathering in which they feel they are doing exactly what they should be doing at that given moment, something beautiful happens. That individual loses track of time and enters a flow state in which all worries about the past and future are filtered out of mind. The sole focus is the present moment and completing a given task to the best of one's abilities.

Purpose is multidimensional and abstract, but I believe it can be achieved by finding the things in life that lead to eudemonic pleasure and stimulate the flow state. I experience flow when I spend time with family, when I step on a tennis court, and when I am studying the mind and brain with the aim of helping individuals to improve their lives. I approach these tasks with great care, and I try to spend a large portion of my life engaged in each of them. It is difficult to find purpose yet frustratingly easy to lose it, especially in times of high stress, immense change, and physical illness. However, I firmly believe that purpose can never truly be lost, but only misplaced. Such times of turmoil and suffering can lead to some of our most meaningful insights and revolutions. With the right mindset, lifestyle habits, and intervention tools, purpose (if properly pursued) can always be found again. In the words of the great Viktor Frankl "What is to give light must endure burning"

References

1. Tooby, J. (2018). The emergence of evolutionary psychology. In *Emerging syntheses in science* (pp. 67-76). CRC Press.

2. Maslow, A., & Lewis, K. J. (1987). Maslow's hierarchy of needs. *Salenger Incorporated, 14*(17), 987-990.

3. Marrero, L. A. (2013). *The path to a meaningful purpose: Psychological foundations of logoteleology.* iUniverse.

4. Klinger, E. (1998). *The search for meaning in evolutionary perspective and its clinical implications.* Lawrence Erlbaum Associates Publishers.

5. Smaers, J. B., & Soligo, C. (2013). Brain reorganization, not relative brain size, primarily characterizes anthropoid brain evolution. *Proceedings of the Royal Society B: Biological Sciences, 280*(1759), 20130269.

6. Bjorklund, D. F., & Harnishfeger, K. K. (1995). The evolution of inhibition mechanisms and their role in human cognition and behavior. In *Interference and inhibition in cognition* (pp. 141-173). Academic Press.

7. Frankl, V. E. (1945). *Man's search for meaning.* Simon and Schuster.

8. Frankl, V. E. (2017). *Man's Search for Meaning: Young Adult Edition: Young Adult Edition.* Beacon Press.

9. Duckworth, A. L., Steen, T. A., & Seligman, M. E. (2005). Positive psychology in clinical practice. *Annual review of clinical psychology, 1*(1), 629-651.

10. Newell, S. A., Sanson-Fisher, R. W., & Savolainen, N. J. (2002). Systematic review of psychological therapies for cancer patients: overview and recommendations for future research. *Journal of the National Cancer Institute, 94*(8), 558-584.

11. Nagel, T. (2016). IX. Altruism: The Intuitive Issue. In *The Possibility of Altruism* (pp. 79-89). Princeton University Press.

12. Markway, B., & Markway, G. (2003). *Painfully shy: How to overcome social anxiety and reclaim your life.* Macmillan.

13. Harris, R. (2011). *The Confidence Gap.* New Harbinger Publications.

References

14. Outlaw, K., & Rushing, D. S. (2018). Increasing empathy in mental health nursing using simulation and reflective journaling. *Journal of Nursing Education, 57*(12), 766-766.

15. Spreng, R. N., & Grady, C. L. (2010). Patterns of brain activity supporting autobiographical memory, prospection, and theory of mind, and their relationship to the default mode network. *Journal of cognitive neuroscience, 22*(6), 1112-1123.

16. Jeter, D. (2001). *The life you imagine: Life lessons for achieving your dreams.* Crown.

17. Haidt, J. (2006). *The happiness hypothesis: Finding modern truth in ancient wisdom.* Basic books.

18. Mischel, W., Shoda, Y., & Peake, P. K. (1988). The nature of adolescent competencies predicted by preschool delay of gratification. *Journal of personality and social psychology, 54*(4), 687.

19. Mischel, W., Shoda, Y., & Peake, P. K. (1990). Predicting adolescent cognitive and self-regulatory competencies from preschool delay of gratification: Identifying diagnostic conditions. *Developmental psychology, 26*(6), 978.

20. Ayduk, O., Mendoza-Denton, R., Mischel, W., Downey, G., Peake, P. K., & Rodriguez, M. (2000). Regulating the interpersonal self: strategic self-regulation for coping with rejection sensitivity. *Journal of personality and social psychology, 79*(5), 776.

21. Casey, B. J., Somerville, L. H., Gotlib, I. H., Ayduk, O., Franklin, N. T., Askren, M. K., ... & Shoda, Y. (2011). Behavioral and neural correlates of delay of gratification 40 years later. *Proceedings of the National Academy of Sciences, 108*(36), 14998-15003.

22. Wood, J., & Ahmari, S. E. (2015). A framework for understanding the emerging role of corticolimbic-ventral striatal networks in OCD-associated repetitive behaviors. *Frontiers in systems neuroscience, 9*, 171.

23. Miyake, A., Friedman, N. P., Emerson, M. J., Witzki, A. H., Howerter, A., & Wager, T. D. (2000). The unity and diversity of executive functions and their contributions to complex "frontal lobe" tasks: A latent variable analysis. *Cognitive psychology, 41*(1), 49-100.

References

24. Fleischman, J. (2002). *Phineas Gage: A gruesome but true story about brain science.* Houghton Mifflin Harcourt.

25. Han, Y., & Adolphs, R. (2020). Estimating the heritability of psychological measures in the Human Connectome Project dataset. *PloS one, 15*(7), e0235860.

26. Saveanu, R. V., & Nemeroff, C. B. (2012). Etiology of depression: genetic and environmental factors. *Psychiatric clinics, 35*(1), 51-71.

27. Pribram, K. H. (1973). The primate frontal cortex–executive of the brain. In *Psychophysiology of the frontal lobes* (pp. 293-314). Academic Press.

28. Lee, R. R., Ward, A. R., Lane, D. M., Aman, M. G., Loveland, K. A., Mansour, R., & Pearson, D. A. (2021). Executive function in autism: Association with ADHD and ASD symptoms. *Journal of Autism and Developmental Disorders*, 1-13.

29. Heffernan, M., Andrews, G., Fiatarone Singh, M. A., Valenzuela, M., Anstey, K. J., Maeder, A. J., ... & Brodaty, H. (2019). Maintain your brain: protocol of a 3-year randomized controlled trial of a personalized multi-modal digital health intervention to prevent cognitive decline among community dwelling 55 to 77 year olds. *Journal of Alzheimer's disease, 70*(s1), S221-S237.

30. Zelazo, P. D. (2020). Executive function and psychopathology: A neurodevelopmental perspective. *Annual review of clinical psychology, 16*(1), 431-454.

31. Baddeley, A. (2000). The episodic buffer: a new component of working memory?. *Trends in cognitive sciences, 4*(11), 417-423.

32. Guarino, A., Favieri, F., Boncompagni, I., Agostini, F., Cantone, M., & Casagrande, M. (2019). Executive functions in Alzheimer disease: a systematic review. *Frontiers in aging neuroscience, 10*, 437.

33. Zainal, N. H., & Newman, M. G. (2022). Depression and worry symptoms predict future executive functioning impairment via inflammation. *Psychological Medicine, 52*(15), 3625-3635.

34. Peretz, C., Korczyn, A. D., Shatil, E., Aharonson, V., Birnboim, S., & Giladi, N. (2011). Computer-based, personalized cognitive training versus classical

References

computer games: a randomized double-blind prospective trial of cognitive stimulation. *Neuroepidemiology, 36*(2), 91-99.

35. Shatil, E., Mikulecka, J., Bellotti, F., & Bureš, V. (2014). Novel television-based cognitive training improves working memory and executive function. *PloS one, 9*(7), e101472.

36. Apter, B. J. (2012). Do computerised training programmes designed to improve working memory work?. *Educational Psychology in Practice, 28*(3), 257-272.

37. Jaeggi, S. M., Buschkuehl, M., Jonides, J., & Perrig, W. J. (2008). Improving fluid intelligence with training on working memory. *Proceedings of the National Academy of Sciences, 105*(19), 6829-6833.

38. Jaeggi, S. M., Studer-Luethi, B., Buschkuehl, M., Su, Y. F., Jonides, J., & Perrig, W. J. (2010). The relationship between n-back performance and matrix reasoning—implications for training and transfer. *Intelligence, 38*(6), 625-635.

39. Salminen, T., Mårtensson, J., Schubert, T., & Kühn, S. (2016). Increased integrity of white matter pathways after dual n-back training. *Neuroimage, 133*, 244-250.

40. Salminen, T., Forlim, C. G., Schubert, T., & Kühn, S. (2020). Dual n-back training improves functional connectivity of the right inferior frontal gyrus at rest. *Scientific reports, 10*(1), 1-10.

41. Ansari, T. L., & Derakshan, N. (2011). The neural correlates of impaired inhibitory control in anxiety. *Neuropsychologia, 49*(5), 1146-1153.

42. Schweizer, S., Grahn, J., Hampshire, A., Mobbs, D., & Dalgleish, T. (2013). Training the emotional brain: improving affective control through emotional working memory training. *Journal of Neuroscience, 33*(12), 5301-5311.

43. Larsen, S. E., Lotfi, S., Bennett, K. P., Larson, C. L., Dean-Bernhoft, C., & Lee, H. J. (2019). A pilot randomized trial of a dual n-back emotional working memory training program for veterans with elevated PTSD symptoms. *Psychiatry research, 275*, 261-268.

44. Diamond, A. (2012). Activities and programs that improve children's executive functions. *Current directions in psychological science, 21*(5), 335-341.

References

45. Vetter, C., Chang, S. C., Devore, E. E., Rohrer, F., Okereke, O. I., & Schernhammer, E. S. (2018). Prospective study of chronotype and incident depression among middle-and older-aged women in the Nurses' Health Study II. *Journal of psychiatric research*, *103*, 156-160.

46. Randler, C., & Schaal, S. (2010). Morningness–eveningness, habitual sleep-wake variables and cortisol level. *Biological psychology*, *85*(1), 14-18.

47. Roenneberg, T., Wirz-Justice, A., & Merrow, M. (2003). Life between clocks: daily temporal patterns of human chronotypes. *Journal of biological rhythms*, *18*(1), 80-90.

48. Finkel, E. J., Bail, C. A., Cikara, M., Ditto, P. H., Iyengar, S., Klar, S., ... & Druckman, J. N. (2020). Political sectarianism in America. *Science*, *370*(6516), 533-536.

49. Ma, S. C., Wang, H. H., & Chien, T. W. (2017). A new technique to measure online bullying: online computerized adaptive testing. *Annals of general psychiatry*, *16*(1), 1-10.

50. Lembke, A. (2021). *Dopamine nation: Finding balance in the age of indulgence*. Penguin.

51. Kedia, G., Mussweiler, T., & Linden, D. E. (2014). Brain mechanisms of social comparison and their influence on the reward system. *Neuroreport*, *25*(16), 1255.

52. Mortimer, J. A., & Stern, Y. (2019). Physical exercise and activity may be important in reducing dementia risk at any age. *Neurology*, *92*(8), 362-363.

53. Blumenthal, J. A., Smith, P. J., Mabe, S., Hinderliter, A., Lin, P. H., Liao, L., ... & Sherwood, A. (2019). Lifestyle and neurocognition in older adults with cognitive impairments: A randomized trial. *Neurology*, *92*(3), e212-e223.

54. Stroth, S., Kubesch, S., Dieterle, K., Ruchsow, M., Heim, R., & Kiefer, M. (2009). Physical fitness, but not acute exercise modulates event-related potential indices for executive control in healthy adolescents. *Brain research*, *1269*, 114-124.

55. Stern, Y., MacKay-Brandt, A., Lee, S., McKinley, P., McIntyre, K., Razlighi, Q., ... & Sloan, R. P. (2019). Effect of aerobic exercise on cognition in younger adults: A randomized clinical trial. *Neurology*, *92*(9), e905-e916.

References

56. Borrega-Mouquinho, Y., Sánchez-Gómez, J., Fuentes-García, J. P., Collado-Mateo, D., & Villafaina, S. (2021). Effects of high-intensity interval training and moderate-intensity training on stress, depression, anxiety, and resilience in healthy adults during coronavirus disease 2019 confinement: a randomized controlled trial. *Frontiers in Psychology*, *12*, 643069.

57. Li, L., Wang, H., Luo, H., Zhang, X., Zhang, R., & Li, X. (2020). Interpersonal neural synchronization during cooperative behavior of basketball players: a fNIRS-based hyperscanning study. *Frontiers in human neuroscience*, *14*, 169.

58. Matt, S. M., & Gaskill, P. J. (2020). Where is dopamine and how do immune cells see it?: dopamine-mediated immune cell function in health and disease. *Journal of Neuroimmune Pharmacology*, *15*(1), 114-164.

59. Meder, D., Herz, D. M., Rowe, J. B., Lehéricy, S., & Siebner, H. R. (2019). The role of dopamine in the brain-lessons learned from Parkinson's disease. *Neuroimage*, *190*, 79-93.

60. Florea, M., Rodaros, D., Poirier, I., Daneault, C., Des Rosiers, C., ... & Fulton, S. (2016). Dampened mesolimbic dopamine function and signaling by saturated but not monounsaturated dietary lipids. *Neuropsychopharmacology*, *41*(3), 811-821.

61. Lampariello, L. R., Cortelazzo, A., Guerranti, R., Sticozzi, C., & Valacchi, G. (2012). The magic velvet bean of Mucuna pruriens. *Journal of traditional and complementary medicine*, *2*(4), 331-339.

62. Ikram, M., Park, T. J., Ali, T., & Kim, M. O. (2020). Antioxidant and neuroprotective effects of caffeine against Alzheimer's and Parkinson's disease: Insight into the role of Nrf-2 and A2AR signaling. *Antioxidants*, *9*(9), 902.

63. Pham, D. L., Mashayekh, A., Yousem, D. M., Dizon, M., Barker, P. B., & Lin, D. D. (2011). Effects of Ginkgo biloba on cerebral blood flow assessed by quantitative MR perfusion imaging: a pilot study. *Neuroradiology*, *53*(3), 185-191.

64. Spasov, A. A., Wikman, G. K., Mandrikov, V. B., Mironova, I. A., & Neumoin, V. V. (2000). A double-blind, placebo-controlled pilot study of the stimulating and adaptogenic effect of Rhodiola rosea SHR-5 extract on the

fatigue of students caused by stress during an examination period with a repeated low-dose regimen. *Phytomedicine, 7*(2), 85-89.

65. Lindseth, G., Helland, B., & Caspers, J. (2015). The effects of dietary tryptophan on affective disorders. *Archives of psychiatric nursing, 29*(2), 102-107.

66. Reuter, M., Zamoscik, V., Plieger, T., Bravo, R., Ugartemendia, L., Rodriguez, A. B., & Kirsch, P. (2021). Tryptophan-rich diet is negatively associated with depression and positively linked to social cognition. *Nutrition Research, 85,* 14-20.

67. Kikuchi, A. M., Tanabe, A., & Iwahori, Y. (2021). A systematic review of the effect of L-tryptophan supplementation on mood and emotional functioning. *Journal of dietary supplements, 18*(3), 316-333.

68. Mueller, P. S., Plevak, D. J., & Rummans, T. A. (2001, December). Religious involvement, spirituality, and medicine: implications for clinical practice. In *Mayo clinic proceedings* (Vol. 76, No. 12, pp. 1225-1235). Elsevier.

69. Jones, J. M. (2021). US church membership falls below majority for first time. *Gallup News.*

70. Lipka, M., & Gecewicz, C. (2017). More Americans now say they're spiritual but not religious.

71. Holiday, R. (2014). *The obstacle is the way: The timeless art of turning trials into triumph.* Penguin.

72. Scheier, M. F., Wrosch, C., Baum, A., Cohen, S., Martire, L. M., Matthews, K. A., ... & Zdaniuk, B. (2006). The life engagement test: Assessing purpose in life. *Journal of behavioral medicine, 29*(3), 291-298.

73. Hill, P. L., Cheung, F., Kube, A., & Burrow, A. L. (2019). Life engagement is associated with higher GDP among societies. *Journal of research in personality, 78,* 210-214.

74. Shahnaz, I., & Karim, A. R. (2014). The impact of Internet addiction on life satisfaction and life engagement in young adults. *Universal Journal of Psychology, 2*(9), 273-284.

75. Crumbaugh, J. C. (1968). Cross-validation of purpose-in-life test based on Frankl's concepts. *Journal of individual psychology, 24*(1), 74.

References

76. Yarnell, T. D. (1971). Purpose-in-Life Test: Further correlates. *Journal of Individual Psychology*.

77. Pearson, P. R., & Sheffield, B. F. (1974). Purpose-in-life and the Eysenck personality inventory. *Journal of Clinical Psychology*.

78. Harlow, L. L., Newcomb, M. D., & Bentler, P. M. (1986). Depression, self-derogation, substance use, and suicide ideation: Lack of purpose in life as a mediational factor. *Journal of clinical psychology*, *42*(1), 5-21.

79. Molasso, W. R. (2006). Exploring Frankl's Purpose in Life with College Students1. *Journal of College and Character*, *7*(1), 1-10.

80. Gutkin, P. M., Fero, K. E., Jacobson, C. E., Chen, J. J., Liang, R. V., Kolar, C., ... & Horst, K. C. (2020). Health mindset is associated with anxiety and depression in patients undergoing treatment for breast cancer.

81. Howe, L. C., Leibowitz, K. A., Perry, M. A., Bitler, J. M., Block, W., Kaptchuk, T. J., ... & Crum, A. J. (2019). Changing patient Mindsets about Non–Life-Threatening symptoms during oral immunotherapy: a randomized clinical trial. *The Journal of Allergy and Clinical Immunology: In Practice*, *7*(5), 1550-1559.

82. Smith, E. N., Young, M. D., & Crum, A. J. (2020). Stress, mindsets, and success in Navy SEALs special warfare training. *Frontiers in psychology*, *10*, 2962.

83. Crum, A. J., & Langer, E. J. (2007). Mind-set matters: Exercise and the placebo effect. *Psychological science*, *18*(2), 165-171.

84. Crum, A. J., Corbin, W. R., Brownell, K. D., & Salovey, P. (2011). Mind over milkshakes: mindsets, not just nutrients, determine ghrelin response. *Health Psychology*, *30*(4), 424.

85. Boyle, P. A., Buchman, A. S., Barnes, L. L., & Bennett, D. A. (2010). Effect of a purpose in life on risk of incident Alzheimer disease and mild cognitive impairment in community-dwelling older persons. *Archives of general psychiatry*, *67*(3), 304-310.

86. Boyle, P. A., Yu, L., Wilson, R. S., Levine, S. R., Schneider, J. A., & Bennett, D. A. (2015). Purpose in life and cerebral infarcts in community-dwelling older people. *Stroke*, *46*(4), 1071-1076.

87. Boyle, P. A., Buchman, A. S., Barnes, L. L., & Bennett, D. A. (2010). Effect of a purpose in life on risk of incident Alzheimer disease and mild cognitive

References

impairment in community-dwelling older persons. *Archives of general psychiatry, 67*(3), 304-310.

88. Kim, E. S., Sun, J. K., Park, N., Kubzansky, L. D., & Peterson, C. (2013). Purpose in life and reduced risk of myocardial infarction among older US adults with coronary heart disease: a two-year follow-up. *Journal of behavioral medicine, 36*(2), 124-133.

89. Koizumi, M., Ito, H., Kaneko, Y., & Motohashi, Y. (2008). Effect of having a sense of purpose in life on the risk of death from cardiovascular diseases. *Journal of epidemiology*, 0808270028-0808270028.

90. Friedman, E. M., Hayney, M., Love, G. D., Singer, B. H., & Ryff, C. D. (2007). Plasma interleukin-6 and soluble IL-6 receptors are associated with psychological well-being in aging women. *Health Psychology, 26*(3), 305.

91. Guimond, A. J., Shiba, K., Kim, E. S., & Kubzansky, L. D. (2022). Sense of purpose in life and inflammation in healthy older adults: A longitudinal study. *Psychoneuroendocrinology, 141*, 105746.

92. Huta, V. (2013). Pursuing eudaimonia versus hedonia: Distinctions, similarities, and relationships.

93. Costa, V. D., Lang, P. J., Sabatinelli, D., Versace, F., & Bradley, M. M. (2010). Emotional imagery: assessing pleasure and arousal in the brain's reward circuitry. *Human brain mapping, 31*(9), 1446-1457.

94. Davidson, R. J., & Schuyler, B. S. (2015). Neuroscience of happiness. *World happiness report*, 88-105.

95. Heller, A. S., Johnstone, T., Shackman, A. J., Light, S. N., Peterson, M. J., Kolden, G. G., ... & Davidson, R. J. (2009). Reduced capacity to sustain positive emotion in major depression reflects diminished maintenance of fronto-striatal brain activation. *Proceedings of the National Academy of Sciences, 106*(52), 22445-22450.

96. Telzer, E. H. (2016). Dopaminergic reward sensitivity can promote adolescent health: A new perspective on the mechanism of ventral striatum activation. *Developmental cognitive neuroscience, 17*, 57-67.

References

97. Wang, M., Perova, Z., Arenkiel, B. R., & Li, B. (2014). Synaptic modifications in the medial prefrontal cortex in susceptibility and resilience to stress. *Journal of Neuroscience, 34*(22), 7485-7492.

98. Covington, H. E., Lobo, M. K., Maze, I., Vialou, V., Hyman, J. M., Zaman, S., ... & Nestler, E. J. (2010). Antidepressant effect of optogenetic stimulation of the medial prefrontal cortex. *Journal of Neuroscience, 30*(48), 16082-16090.

99. Everaerd, D., Klumpers, F., van Wingen, G., Tendolkar, I., & Fernández, G. (2015). Association between neuroticism and amygdala responsivity emerges under stressful conditions. *Neuroimage, 112,* 218-224.

100. Iverach, L., Menzies, R. G., & Menzies, R. E. (2014). Death anxiety and its role in psychopathology: Reviewing the status of a transdiagnostic construct. *Clinical psychology review, 34*(7), 580-593.

101. Lichtenstein, P., & Annas, P. (2000). Heritability and prevalence of specific fears and phobias in childhood. *The Journal of Child Psychology and Psychiatry and Allied Disciplines, 41*(7), 927-937.

102. Ryff, C. D., Heller, A. S., Schaefer, S. M., Van Reekum, C., & Davidson, R. J. (2016). Purposeful engagement, healthy aging, and the brain. *Current behavioral neuroscience reports, 3*(4), 318-327.

103. Meng, W., Adams, M. J., Reel, P., Rajendrakumar, A., Huang, Y., Deary, I. J., ... & Smith, B. H. (2020). Genetic correlations between pain phenotypes and depression and neuroticism. *European Journal of Human Genetics, 28*(3), 358-366.

104. Pradhan, M., Chettri, A., & Maheshwari, S. (2022). Fear of death in the shadow of COVID-19: The mediating role of perceived stress in the relationship between neuroticism and death anxiety. *Death Studies, 46*(5), 1106-1110.

105. Amen, D. G. (2020). *The End of Mental Illness: How Neuroscience is Transforming Psychiatry and Helping Prevent Or Reverse Mood and Anxiety Disorders, ADHD, Addictions, PTSD, Psychosis, Personality Disorders, and More.* Tyndale Momentum.

106. Reznik, S. J., & Allen, J. J. (2018). Frontal asymmetry as a mediator and moderator of emotion: An updated review. *Psychophysiology, 55*(1), e12965.

References

107. Hackett, N. (2018). QEEG phenotypes, depression and TMS. *Progress in Neurology and Psychiatry*, *22*(3), 23-26.

108. Kirsch, I. (2010). *The emperor's new drugs: Exploding the antidepressant myth.* ReadHowYouWant. com.

109. Hari, J. (2018). *Lost connections.* Bloomsbury publishing.

110. Cipriani, A., Furukawa, T. A., Salanti, G., Chaimani, A., Atkinson, L. Z., Ogawa, Y., ... & Geddes, J. R. (2018). Comparative efficacy and acceptability of 21 antidepressant drugs for the acute treatment of adults with major depressive disorder: a systematic review and network meta-analysis. *Focus*, *16*(4), 420-429.

111. Rush, A. J., Warden, D., Wisniewski, S. R., Fava, M., Trivedi, M. H., Gaynes, B. N., & Nierenberg, A. A. (2009). Star* d. *CNS drugs*, *23*(8), 627-647.

112. Cascade, E., Kalali, A. H., & Kennedy, S. H. (2009). Real-world data on SSRI antidepressant side effects. *Psychiatry (Edgmont)*, *6*(2), 16.

113. Zangen, A., Roth, Y., Voller, B., & Hallett, M. (2005). Transcranial magnetic stimulation of deep brain regions: evidence for efficacy of the H-coil. *Clinical neurophysiology*, *116*(4), 775-779.

114. Noda, Y., Silverstein, W. K., Barr, M. S., Vila-Rodriguez, F., Downar, J., Rajji, T. K., ... & Blumberger, D. M. (2015). Neurobiological mechanisms of repetitive transcranial magnetic stimulation of the dorsolateral prefrontal cortex in depression: a systematic review. *Psychological medicine*, *45*(16), 3411-3432.

115. Filipčić, I., Filipčić, I. Š., Milovac, Ž., Sučić, S., Gajšak, T., Ivezić, E., ... & Heilig, M. (2019). Efficacy of repetitive transcranial magnetic stimulation using a figure-8-coil or an H1-Coil in treatment of major depressive disorder; A randomized clinical trial. *Journal of Psychiatric Research*, *114*, 113-119.

116. Tendler, A., Harmelech, T., Gersner, R., & Roth, Y. (2021). Seizures provoked by H-coils from 2010 to 2020. *Brain stimulation: basic, translational, and clinical Research in neuromodulation*, *14*(1), 66-68.

117. Skowron, D. M., & Stimmel, G. L. (1992). Antidepressants and the risk of seizures. *Pharmacotherapy: The Journal of Human Pharmacology and Drug Therapy*, *12*(1), 18-22.

References

118. Pell, G. S., Zibman, S., Roth, Y., Tendler, A., & Zangen, A. (2021). Deep TMS for the treatment of comorbid anxiety. *Brain Stimulation: Basic, Translational, and Clinical Research in Neuromodulation, 14*(5), 1408-1409.

119. Carmi, L., Tendler, A., Bystritsky, A., Hollander, E., Blumberger, D. M., Daskalakis, J., ... & Zohar, J. (2019). Efficacy and safety of deep transcranial magnetic stimulation for obsessive-compulsive disorder: a prospective multicenter randomized double-blind placebo-controlled trial. *American Journal of Psychiatry, 176*(11), 931-938.

120. Zangen, A., Moshe, H., Martinez, D., Barnea-Ygael, N., Vapnik, T., Bystritsky, A., ... & George, M. S. (2021). Repetitive transcranial magnetic stimulation for smoking cessation: a pivotal multicenter double-blind randomized controlled trial. *World Psychiatry, 20*(3), 397-404.

121. Driessen, E., Hollon, S. D., Bockting, C. L., Cuijpers, P., & Turner, E. H. (2015). Does publication bias inflate the apparent efficacy of psychological treatment for major depressive disorder? A systematic review and meta-analysis of US National Institutes of Health-funded trials. *PloS one, 10*(9), e0137864.

122. Frankl, V. E. (1984). *Search for meaning.* Milwaukee, WI, USA: Mount Mary College.

123. Vos, J., & Vitali, D. (2018). The effects of psychological meaning-centered therapies on quality of life and psychological stress: A metaanalysis. *Palliative & supportive care, 16*(5), 608-632.

124. Kang, K. A., Han, S. J., Lim, Y. S., & Kim, S. J. (2019). Meaning-centered interventions for patients with advanced or terminal cancer: a meta-analysis. *Cancer nursing, 42*(4), 332-340.

125. Fereydouni, S., & Forstmeier, S. (2022). An Islamic Form of Logotherapy in the Treatment of Depression, Anxiety and Stress Symptoms in University Students in Iran. *Journal of religion and health, 61*(1), 139-157.

126. Helliwell, J., Layard, R., & Sachs, J. (2018). World happiness report.

127. Csikszentmihalyi, M., Abuhamdeh, S., & Nakamura, J. (2014). Flow. In *Flow and the foundations of positive psychology* (pp. 227-238). Springer, Dordrecht.

References

128. Aston-Jones, G., & Cohen, J. D. (2005). An integrative theory of locus coeruleus-norepinephrine function: adaptive gain and optimal performance. *Annu. Rev. Neurosci.*, *28*, 403-450.

129. Katahira, K., Yamazaki, Y., Yamaoka, C., Ozaki, H., Nakagawa, S., & Nagata, N. (2018). EEG correlates of the flow state: A combination of increased frontal theta and moderate frontocentral alpha rhythm in the mental arithmetic task. *Frontiers in Psychology*, *9*, 300.

130. Shapiro, F. (2014). The role of eye movement desensitization and reprocessing (EMDR) therapy in medicine: addressing the psychological and physical symptoms stemming from adverse life experiences. *The Permanente Journal*, *18*(1), 71.

131. Hebert, R., Lehmann, D., Tan, G., Travis, F., & Arenander, A. (2005). Enhanced EEG alpha time-domain phase synchrony during Transcendental Meditation: Implications for cortical integration theory. *Signal Processing*, *85*(11), 2213-2232.

132. Shanok, N. A., Reive, C., Mize, K. D., & Jones, N. A. (2019). Mindfulness meditation intervention alters neurophysiological symptoms of anxiety and depression in preadolescents. *Journal of Psychophysiology*.

133. Shanok, N. A., Saldias-Manieu, C., Mize, K. D., Chassin, V., & Jones, N. A. (2022). Mindfulness-Training in Preadolescents in School: The Role of Emotionality, EEG in Theta/Beta Bands, Creativity and Attention. *Child Psychiatry & Human Development*, 1-15.

134. Holtmann, M., Sonuga-Barke, E., Cortese, S., & Brandeis, D. (2014). Neurofeedback for ADHD: a review of current evidence. *Child and Adolescent Psychiatric Clinics*, *23*(4), 789-806.

135. Gruzelier, J. H. (2014). EEG-neurofeedback for optimising performance. I: A review of cognitive and affective outcome in healthy participants. *Neuroscience & Biobehavioral Reviews*, *44*, 124-141.

136. Peniston, E. G., & Kulkosky, P. J. (1991). Alpha-theta brainwave neurofeedback for Vietnam veterans with combat-related post-traumatic stress disorder. *Medical Psychotherapy*, *4*(1), 47-60.

References

137. Saxby, E., & Peniston, E. G. (1995). Alpha-theta brainwave neurofeedback training: An effective treatment for male and female alcoholics with depressive symptoms. *Journal of clinical psychology, 51*(5), 685-693.

138. Xiang, M. Q., Hou, X. H., Liao, B. G., Liao, J. W., & Hu, M. (2018). The effect of neurofeedback training for sport performance in athletes: A meta-analysis. *Psychology of Sport and Exercise, 36*, 114-122.

139. Gruzelier, J. H. (2014). EEG-neurofeedback for optimising performance. II: creativity, the performing arts and ecological validity. *Neuroscience & Biobehavioral Reviews, 44*, 142-158.

140. Jesse, R., & Griffiths, R. R. (2014). Psilocybin research at Johns Hopkins: A 2014 report. *Seeking the sacred with psychoactive substances: Chemical paths to spirituality and to god, 2*, 29-43.

141. Griffiths, R. R., Richards, W. A., McCann, U., & Jesse, R. (2006). Psilocybin can occasion mystical-type experiences having substantial and sustained personal meaning and spiritual significance. *Psychopharmacology, 187*(3), 268-283.

142. MacLean, K. A., Johnson, M. W., & Griffiths, R. R. (2011). Mystical experiences occasioned by the hallucinogen psilocybin lead to increases in the personality domain of openness. *Journal of psychopharmacology, 25*(11), 1453-1461.

143. Griffiths, R. R., Richards, W. A., Johnson, M. W., McCann, U. D., & Jesse, R. (2008). Mystical-type experiences occasioned by psilocybin mediate the attribution of personal meaning and spiritual significance 14 months later. *Journal of psychopharmacology, 22*(6), 621-632.

144. Gukasyan, N., Davis, A. K., Barrett, F. S., Cosimano, M. P., Sepeda, N. D., Johnson, M. W., & Griffiths, R. R. (2022). Efficacy and safety of psilocybin-assisted treatment for major depressive disorder: Prospective 12-month follow-up. *Journal of Psychopharmacology, 36*(2), 151-158.

145. Garcia-Romeu, A., R Griffiths, R., & W Johnson, M. (2014). Psilocybin-occasioned mystical experiences in the treatment of tobacco addiction. *Current drug abuse reviews, 7*(3), 157-164.

References

146. Pittenger, C., Bloch, M. H., & Williams, K. (2011). Glutamate abnormalities in obsessive compulsive disorder: neurobiology, pathophysiology, and treatment. *Pharmacology & therapeutics*, *132*(3), 314-332.

147. Suzuki, A., Hara, H., & Kimura, H. (2022). Role of the AMPA receptor in antidepressant effects of ketamine and potential of AMPA receptor potentiators as a novel antidepressant. *Neuropharmacology*, 109308.

148. Onaolapo, A. Y., & Onaolapo, O. J. (2021). Glutamate and depression: Reflecting a deepening knowledge of the gut and brain effects of a ubiquitous molecule. *World Journal of Psychiatry*, *11*(7), 297.

149. McInnes, L. A., Qian, J. J., Gargeya, R. S., DeBattista, C., & Heifets, B. D. (2022). A retrospective analysis of ketamine intravenous therapy for depression in real-world care settings. *Journal of Affective Disorders*, *301*, 486-495.

150. Bahr, R., Lopez, A., & Rey, J. A. (2019). Intranasal esketamine (SpravatoTM) for use in treatment-resistant depression in conjunction with an oral antidepressant. *Pharmacy and Therapeutics*, *44*(6), 340.

151. Liriano, F., Hatten, C., & Schwartz, T. L. (2019). Ketamine as treatment for post-traumatic stress disorder: a review. *Drugs in context, 8*.

152. Nugent, A. C., Ballard, E. D., Gould, T. D., Park, L. T., Moaddel, R., Brutsche, N. E., & Zarate, C. A. (2019). Ketamine has distinct electrophysiological and behavioral effects in depressed and healthy subjects. *Molecular psychiatry*, *24*(7), 1040-1052.

153. Nicol, A. U., & Morton, A. J. (2020). Characteristic patterns of EEG oscillations in sheep (Ovis aries) induced by ketamine may explain the psychotropic effects seen in humans. *Scientific reports*, *10*(1), 1-10.

154. Sleigh, J., Pullon, R. M., Vlisides, P. E., & Warnaby, C. E. (2019). Electroencephalographic slow wave dynamics and loss of behavioural responsiveness induced by ketamine in human volunteers. *British Journal of Anaesthesia*, *123*(5), 592-600.

155. de la Salle, S., Phillips, J. L., Blier, P., & Knott, V. (2022). Electrophysiological correlates and predictors of the antidepressant response to repeated

References

ketamine infusions in treatment-resistant depression. *Progress in Neuro-Psychopharmacology and Biological Psychiatry, 115*, 110507.

156. Musso, F., Brinkmeyer, J., Ecker, D., London, M. K., Thieme, G., Warbrick, T., ... & Winterer, G. (2011). Ketamine effects on brain function—simultaneous fMRI/EEG during a visual oddball task. *Neuroimage, 58*(2), 508-525.